Embroidering the Magic of Plants

HEALING FLOWER, LEAF, AND HERBAL DESIGNS

Yula

Contents

PRESCRIPTION

I

EMBROIDERY TO CHERISH

Page 5

A
Embroidery Hoops

PRESCRIPTION

II

EMBROIDERY TO KEEP CLOSE

Page 10

B
Tote Bags

C
Gusseted Pouches

D
Drawstring Pouches

PRESCRIPTION
III
EMBROIDERY FOR QUIET TIME
Page 19

E
Pincushions

F
Fold-Over Trinket Pouch

G
Glasses Case

H
Pen Case

PRESCRIPTION
IV
WEARABLE EMBROIDERY
Page 23

I
Brooches

Introduction

Thank you for selecting this book among the many books on embroidery that are out there.

My name is Yula, and I started posting my embroidery projects on Instagram. This book is a collection of the projects that have been most popular on that platform. During the pandemic, when we were all spending so much time at home, it seemed many people decided to try their hand at embroidery. All it takes to get started is to stitch a single flower. It's natural to feel discouraged at first, but if you keep working at it, a little each day, your stitches will begin to take shape and align; you'll acquire a few skills; and, before you know it, you might even realize that you've become quite adept at it. That's how it was for me.

I encourage you, readers and embroidery enthusiasts, to pick out your favorite pattern, change up the color scheme, and create your own unique project. There's no question that time spent absorbed in doing something you love is nourishing for the soul.

Slow down, relax, and enjoy yourself as you embroider. Soon enough, your heart will feel refreshed as you realize that this peaceful everyday pastime is always there for you.

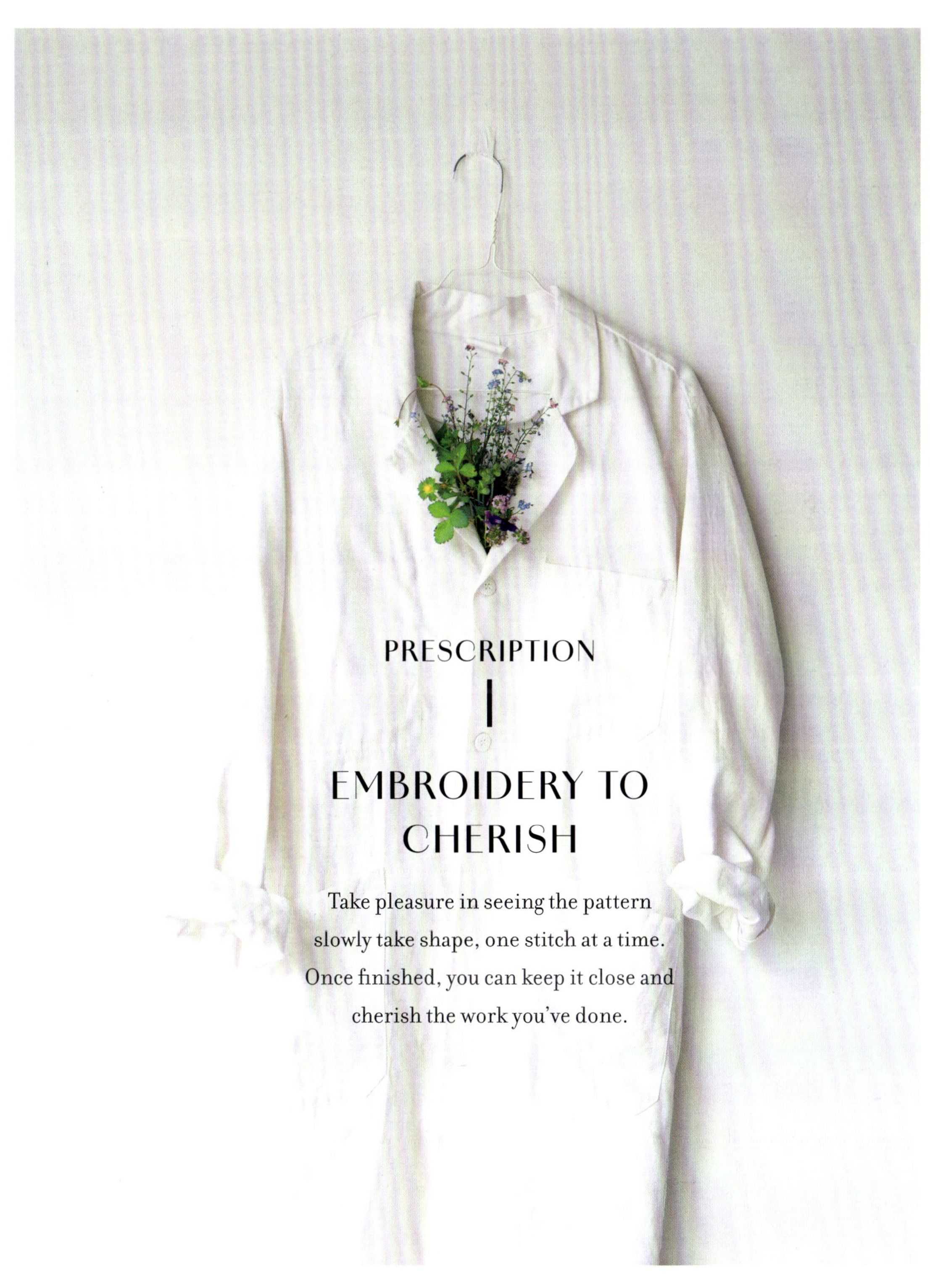

PRESCRIPTION 1

EMBROIDERY TO CHERISH

Take pleasure in seeing the pattern slowly take shape, one stitch at a time. Once finished, you can keep it close and cherish the work you've done.

A

Embroidery Hoops

Instructions p. 39

A round wreath pattern fits perfectly inside this embroidery hoop. Set the wreath size to your own liking.

A-1a Flannel Flowers

Pattern p. 57

A-2 Mimosas

Pattern p. 58

A-3 Blue Daisies

A-4a Flowers on the Breeze

A-5a Floret Wreath

Patterns (in order, from top) pp. 60, 62, 61

A-6 Marguerite Wreath

Pattern p. 64

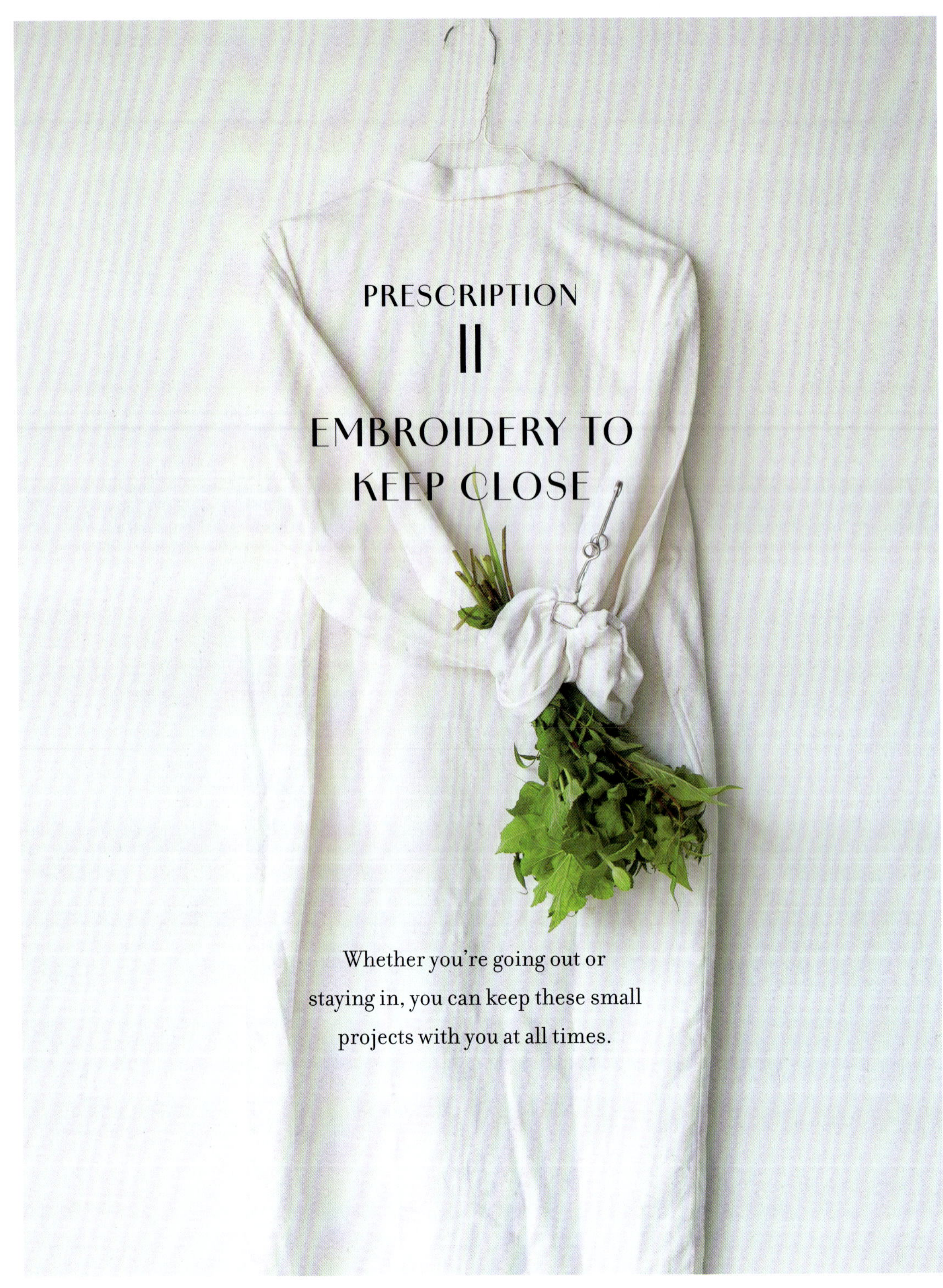

PRESCRIPTION II

EMBROIDERY TO KEEP CLOSE

Whether you're going out or staying in, you can keep these small projects with you at all times.

B

Tote Bags

Instructions p. 40

These simply constructed tote bags are perfect for when you're just stepping out. Choose the size based on the pattern.

B-1 Healing Flowers

Pattern p. 66

B-2 A Walk in the Forest

Pattern p. 67

B-3 A Posy of Marguerites

Pattern p. 70

B-4a Garden Party

Pattern p. 68

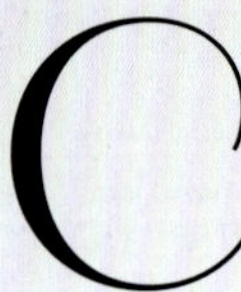

Gusseted Pouches

Instructions p. 42

These cute and round pouches have solid, square bottoms. With such a variety of colors and patterns, you might want to make all of them!

C-1a Forest

C-2a Gentle Breeze

C-3a Wildflowers

C-4a *Jardin*

Patterns (in order, from left to right on opposite page) pp. 75, 76, 77, 78

D-1 Miniature Wreath

D-2 Botanical

D-3 Sunlight

Patterns (in order, from left to right) pp. 79, 80, 81

D

Drawstring Pouches

Instructions p. 44

Flat, nongusseted pouches are easy to make, and you can never have too many. These also make for a thoughtful gift.

D-4a Tree

Pattern p. 82

D-5a, b Bouquet

Pattern p. 83

PRESCRIPTION III

EMBROIDERY FOR QUIET TIME

Calm moments spent at home—
whether sewing, reading, or writing—
are to be treasured.

E

Pincushions

Instructions p. 46

After completing the embroidery design, all you have to do is make a few running stitches and then stuff the cushion with cotton. I put these in little store-bought wooden bowls.

E-a, b, c Garland

Pattern p. 47

F

Fold-Over Trinket Pouch

Instructions p. 48

These are perfect for keeping small valuables, like jewelry or earbuds, safe and sound.

F-a, b, c Pastel Flowers

Pattern p. 49

G
Glasses Case

Instructions p. 50

The glasses case has a rounded bottom, and the pen case has a zipper attached. You're welcome to use them interchangeably.

H
Pen Case

Instructions p. 52

G•H-1a, b Bloom

Pattern p. 84

PRESCRIPTION IV

WEARABLE EMBROIDERY

Adorn yourself with miniature embroideries, just like jewelry or accessories. Swap them out to your liking, whenever you change your outfit or your mood.

I-1a, b, c Nuance

Pattern p. 55

I

Brooches

Instructions p. 54

The tiny flowers are tightly enclosed in these darling little brooches. Discover your own prescription by changing up the color or the pattern.

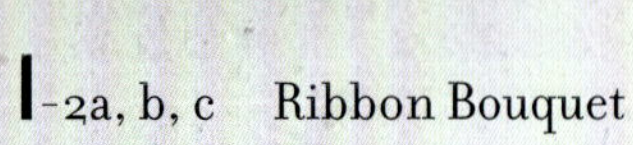

I-2a, b, c Ribbon Bouquet

Pattern p. 87

I-3a, b, c Eternal

Pattern p. 87

I-4a, b, c Crescent

Pattern p. 87

PATTERN SWATCHES
•
COLOR PALETTES

A-1b Flannel Flowers Pattern p. 57

A-5b Floret Wreath Pattern p. 61

A-7a Leaf Wreath Pattern p. 65

A-7b Leaf Wreath

The same project gives a dramatically different impression when you change up the colors or the pattern. Pictured here are a few suggested variations. Use these as inspiration for further creativity to find your favorite.

A-4b Flowers on the Breeze Pattern p. 62

B-5a Field of Trees Pattern p. 71

B-5b Field of Trees

B-6a Marguerites Pattern p. 72

B-6b Marguerites

B-7 Field of Flowers Pattern p. 73

B-8 Paradise Pattern p. 74

B-4b, c, d Garden Party Pattern p. 68

C-1b, c, d Forest

Pattern p. 75

C-2b, c, d Gentle Breeze

Pattern p. 76

C-3b, c, d Wildflowers

Pattern p. 77

C-4b, c, d *Jardin*

Pattern p. 78

D-4b Tree

Pattern p. 82

G•H-2a Hydrangeas Pattern p. 85

G•H-2b, c, d Hydrangeas

G•H-3a, b Rainbow Evergreens Pattern p. 86

LESSONS & HOW TO MAKE

Embroidery Tools

BASIC TOOLS

TOOLS FOR TRACING PATTERNS

USEFUL TOOLS FOR FINISHING PROJECTS

A Scissors: The large scissors are used for fabric and the small scissors are used for cutting out patterns and such. I use *nigiri hasami* snip scissors for cutting embroidery floss and thread.

B Needles: I use French embroidery needles, Nos. 5–7, depending on the number of strands of embroidery floss.

C Needle Threader: This tool makes it easier to put the thread into the eye of a needle.

D Embroidery Floss: For most of the projects in this book, I used DMC No. 25 embroidery floss.

E Embroidery Hoops: This tool is used to stretch fabric tightly. I like to wrap the outer hoop with fabric so that the metal doesn't leave a mark on the fabric.

F Tracer: This tool is used to trace the pattern when transferring onto fabric. You can also use a ballpoint pen that has run out of ink.

G Water-Soluble Fabric Marker: This Chacopen's ink can be erased or washed out.

H & I Tracing Paper and Cellophane: Layer these over patterns when tracing them.

J Embroidery Transfer Paper: I use this paper to transfer patterns onto fabric. The kind branded specifically for embroidery is best.

K Cutting Mat: Place this underneath your work when tracing patterns to avoid damaging the surface of your desk or table.

L Tracing Table/Light Box: When tracing patterns onto white fabric, place the pattern on this to make it transparent.

M Eyeleteer: I like to use this for making neat corners on bags and pouches.

N Bodkin: Use this to thread the drawstrings through casings on a pouch.

O Tailor's Chalk: A powdery chalk variation is useful when drawing long, straight lines.

P Basting Thread: This is helpful for marking the finished edge of patterns with complicated shapes, such as the gusseted pouches.

Q Stay Tape: Use this (0.9-cm diameter) on the opening of a pouch to keep it from losing shape.

Embroidery Basics & Fundamentals

HOW TO HANDLE NO. 25 EMBROIDERY THREAD

No. 25 embroidery thread comes with six strands intertwined. You'll need to separate these fine strands based on the number of strands indicated in the pattern.

1. Pull a standard length of 50–60 cm from the skein, and cut the thread.
2. One at a time, untangle and separate the six strands. They will become twisted again while you are stitching, so continue to untangle them every so often.
3. Arrange the number of strands you need, parallel, with the ends aligned together neatly. Fold the strands over your embroidery needle and then thread them through the eye.

TRACING PATTERNS

First, place tracing paper over the pattern. Next, layer in this order: Place embroidery transfer paper over the fabric followed by the tracing paper, the pattern, and the cellophane. Transfer the pattern.

When transferring the embroidery pattern, it's best to trace the project outlines for the item you're making at the same time to use them as guidelines. It makes it easier to know where to position the embroidery.

STARTING AND ENDING YOUR EMBROIDERY

Generally, I don't make knots in my embroidery. When starting, I leave about 10 cm of thread from the starting point, then I work my stitches. Once I've finished, I clean up by weaving in the ends. The same goes for ending my embroidery. If you're worried about it, feel free to make knots.

• Anchoring the thread vertically
Turn your work over, weave the thread through your stitches two or three times, then trim the end.

• Anchoring the thread horizontally
On the reverse side, pass the thread under your stitches one or two times, then trim the end.

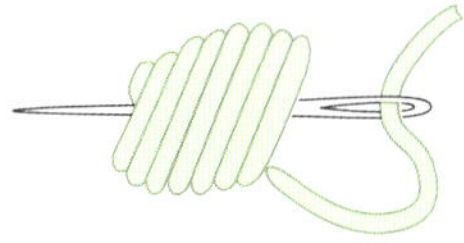

SEQUENCE OF STITCHING

Ideally, the best sequence for stitches is to start by creating outlines so the tracings will not be erased or disappear. Once you have first worked the outlines, you can go back and fill in areas with satin or chain stitches, then finish the finer details. I always work French knot stitches last.

1. For flowers, work the backstitches of the satin stitches (you can go back and work the satin stitches themselves). For leaves, work the stems (outline stitches).
2. For leaves that will be filled in with chain stitches, work only the borders first.
3. Work the branches, twigs, and leaves.

Embroidery Stitches Used in This Book

OUTLINE STITCH

1 Up
3 Up
2 Down
3
Unify your work in this direction.
Repeat steps 2–3.

SATIN STITCH

Once you reach the tip, pass the thread underneath and bring it back up to begin stitching the other half.
Backstitches
Down
3 Up
c
2 Down
1 Up
b
a
Up
Down
To set the direction of the stitches, it helps to start from the widest point.
Repeat steps 2–3.

*Create volume by working backstitches inside the tracings and then filling in with satin stitches.

STRAIGHT STITCH

CHAIN STITCH

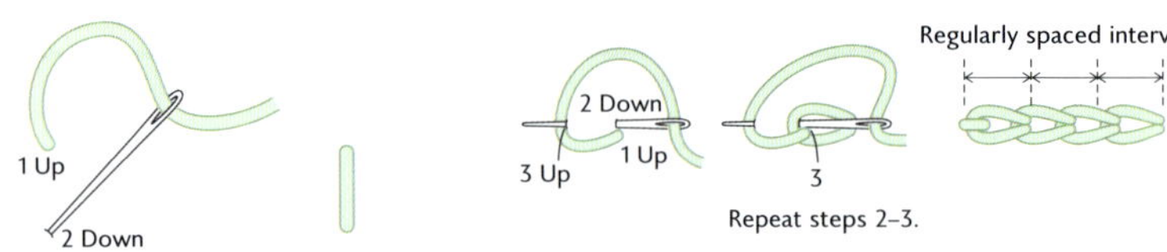

BACKSTITCH

3 Up
1 Up
2 Down
5 Up
3
4 Down (1)

FISHBONE STITCH

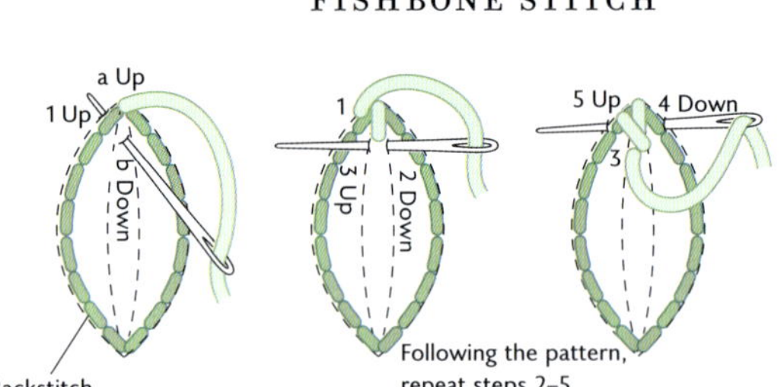

*Create volume by working backstitches inside the tracings and then filling in with satin stitches.

FRENCH KNOT STITCH (DOUBLE WRAP)

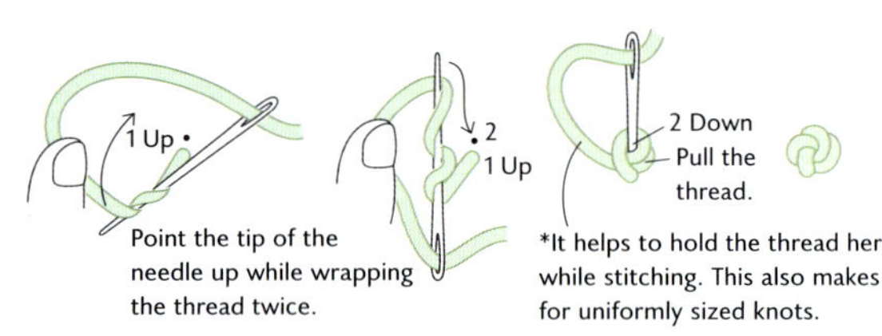

RUNNING STITCH

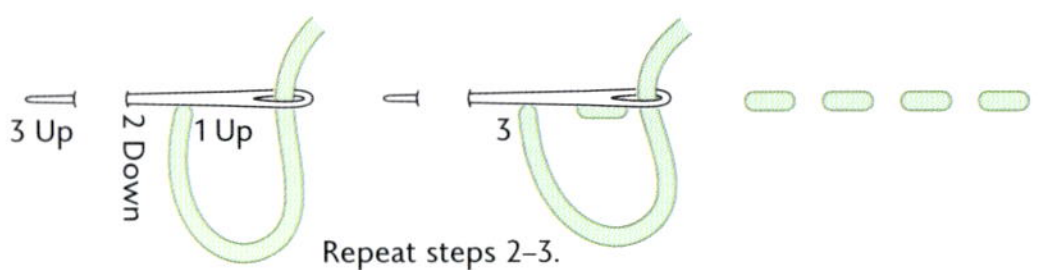

LAZY DAISY STITCH

Working straight stitch over lazy daisy stitch

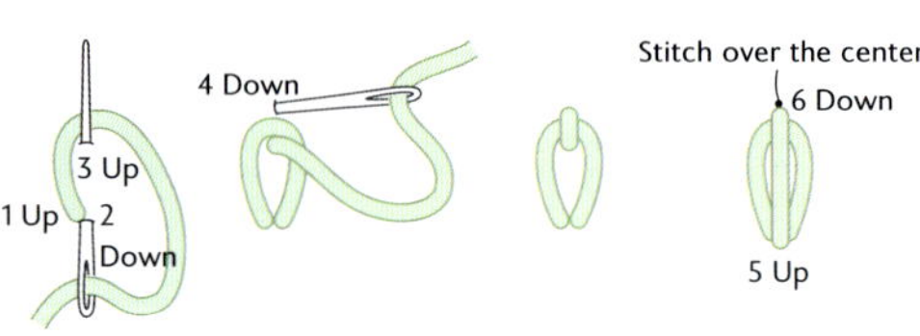

*Create plumply shaped leaves by pulling the thread taut.

Stitching Tips

HOW TO CREATE SHADING ON FLOWER PETALS

Use satin stitches to create gradations of color on flower petals.

1. Once you've completed the outline with backstitches, add guiding lines that lead toward the center.

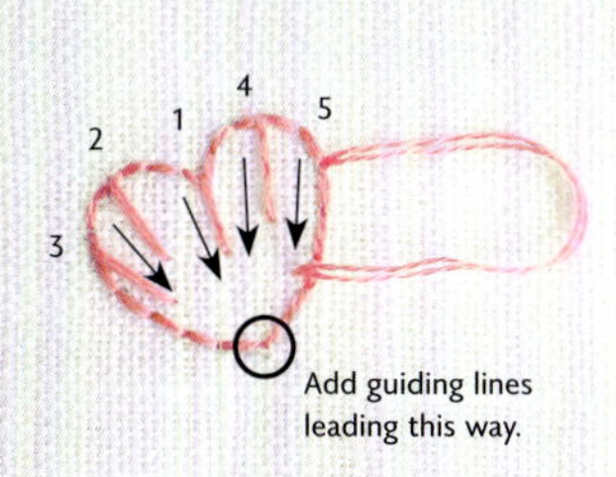

2. Work outward from step 1, filling in the area with satin stitches.

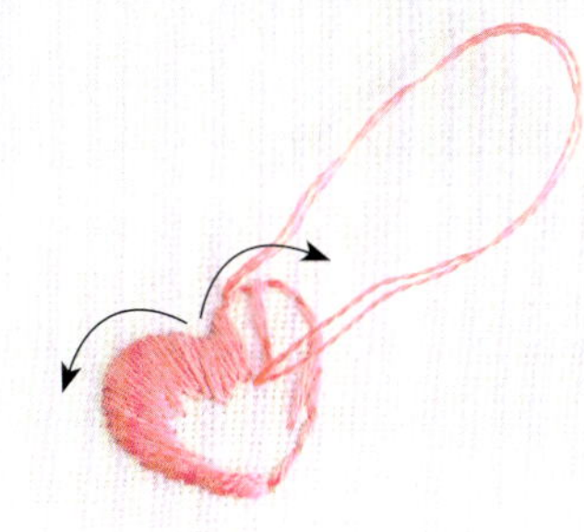

3. For the inner part, add similar guiding lines that lead toward the center.

4. Work long and short straight stitches in a zigzag pattern.

HOW TO STITCH MINIATURE ROSES

Create miniature roses by layering stitches that mimic tiny petals.

1. Work the center with straight stitches.

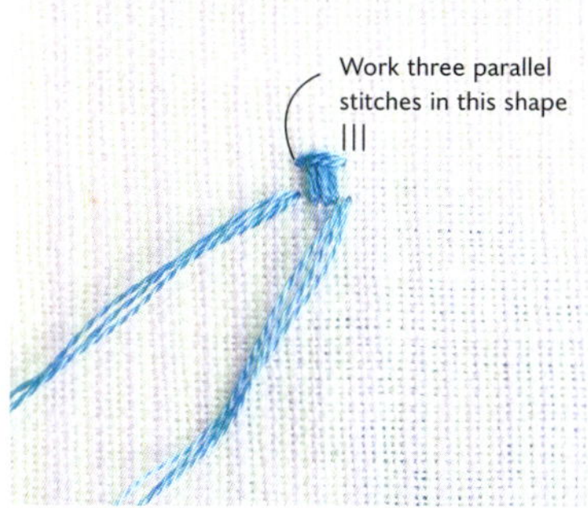

2. Add straight stitches at each corner.

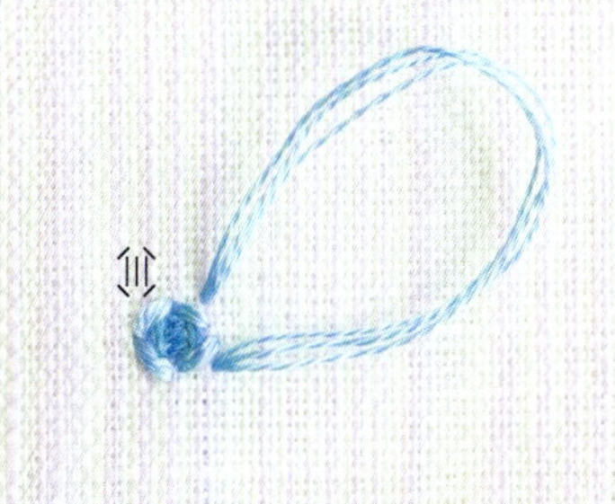

3. Once the shape starts to round, add outline stitches.

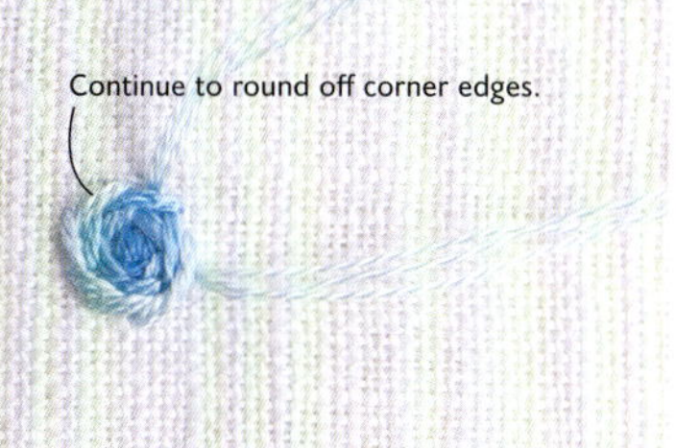

Stitching Tips

CREATING CONVEXITY

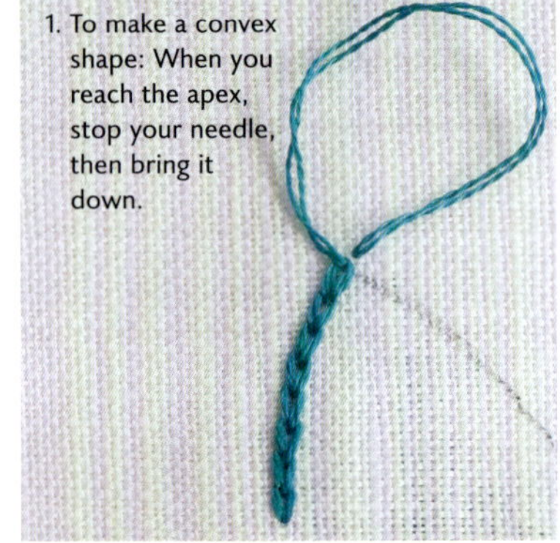

2. Bring the needle back up, creating an acute angle, then continue stitching.

HOW TO CREATE TEXTURE WITH CHAIN STITCHES

CREATING CONCAVITY

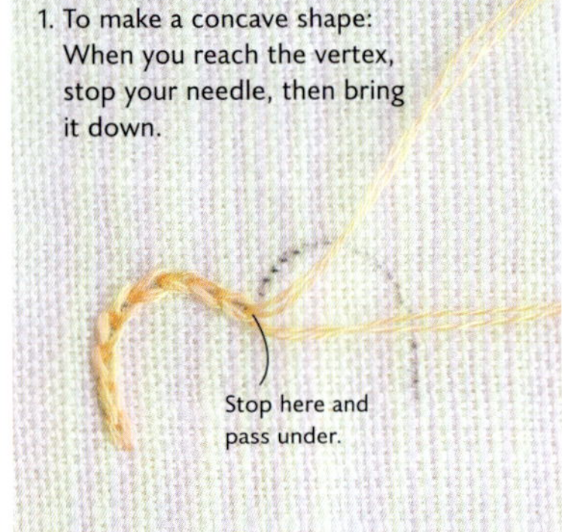

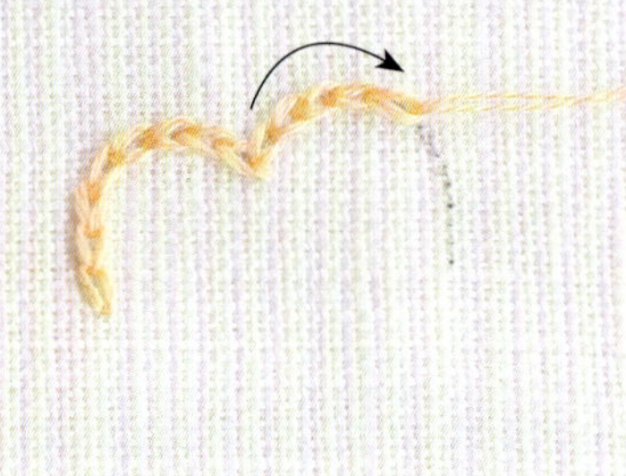

A Embroidery Hoops

Projects pp. 6–9, 27 • Patterns pp. 57–65
Finished measurements: Small, 15-cm diameter, Large, 25-cm diameter

Materials
No. 25 embroidery floss (colors listed on pattern pages)
Fabric Small (A-1, 3, 5, 6, 7): Linen, 25 x 25 cm
Large (A-2, 4): Linen, 35 x 35 cm
Other: Backing fabric, embroidery hoop

1. Work embroidery on the exterior fabric.

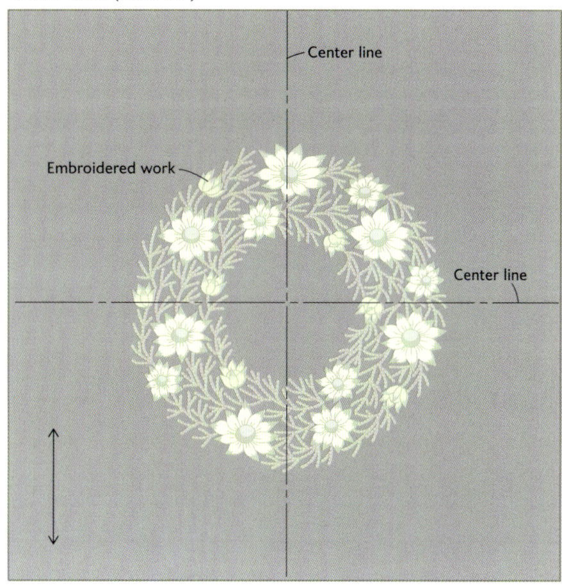

2. Layer exterior fabric over the backing fabric.

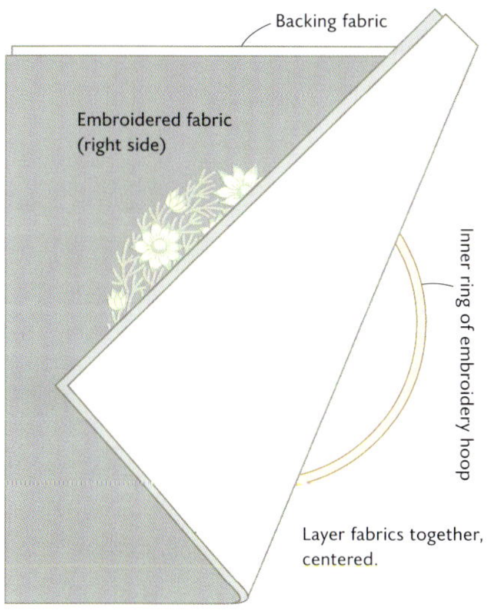

3. Fasten outer ring, then cut fabric, leaving about a 4-cm seam allowance all around.

4. Gather the edges of the seam allowance by sewing together on reverse side.

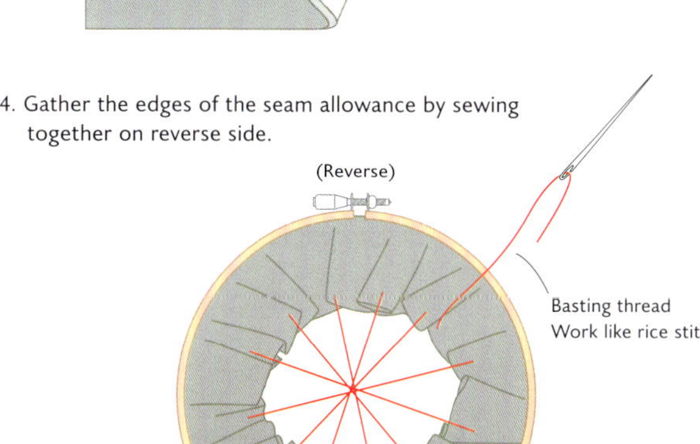

Finished project (small)

B Tote Bags

Projects pp. 11–13, 28–29 • Patterns pp. 66–74
Finished measurements: Refer to patterns (see p. 56 for pattern reading key)

Materials
No. 25 embroidery floss (colors listed on pattern pages)
Fabric

		Exterior fabric (linen)	Lining fabric (cotton)	Other (fusible interfacing)
a	B-4, 7	100 x 45 cm	70 x 30 cm	40 x 30 cm
b	B-5, 6	90 x 35 cm	60 x 25 cm	40 x 30 cm
c	B-3	85 x 35 cm	60 x 20 cm	35 x 30 cm
d	B-2, 8	95 x 35 cm	65 x 25 cm	40 x 30 cm
e	B-1	70 x 25 cm	45 x 20 cm	35 x 25 cm

*Add a 1-cm seam allowance, unless noted otherwise.

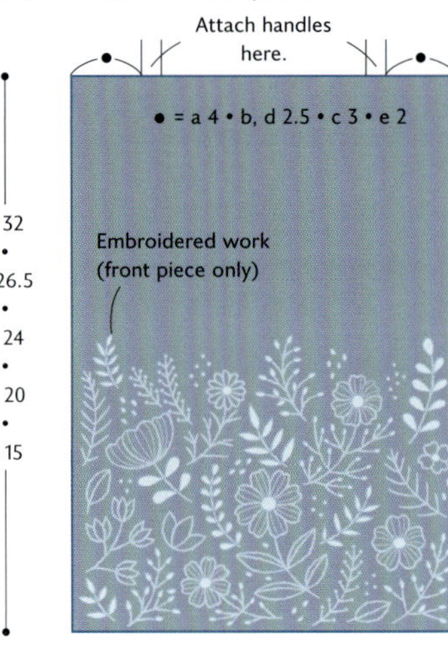

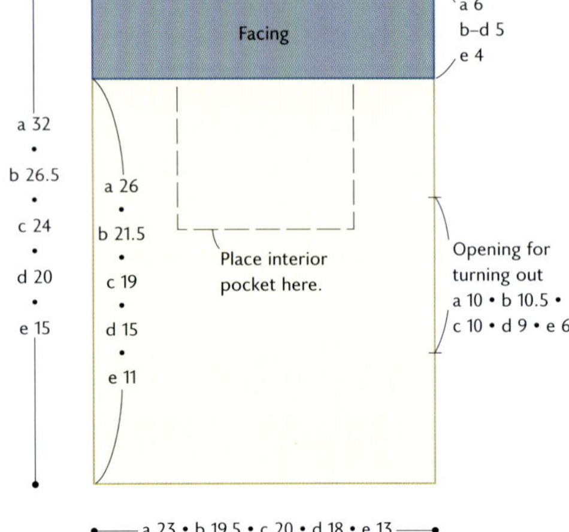

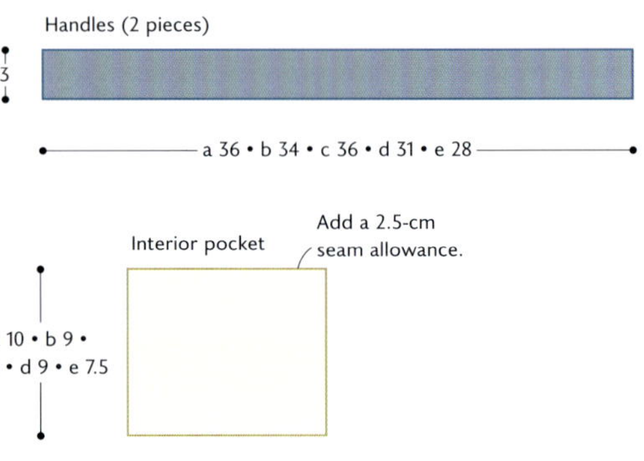

1. Work embroidery on the front side of the exterior fabric.

2. Cut fabric for each part, adding a 1-cm seam allowance all around, and attach fusible interfacing.

1
Attach fusible interfacing.
Handle (reverse side)
1
Facing (reverse side)
Attach fusible interfacing.
2.5
Interior pocket (reverse side)
Secure with lockstitch or zigzag machine stitch.
1

3. Attach facing and interior pocket to lining fabric.

1
Right sides together
Sew.
Facing (reverse side)
Lining fabric (right side)

Using an iron, press a 1.5-cm triple fold along the opening of the pocket.
1
Machine stitch.
Fold the seam allowances this way.

Machine stitch.
Facing (right side)
Opening of pocket
Align with center.
Interior pocket (right side)
0.2
Lining fabric (right side)
Tuck the seam allowances underneath.

4. Make the handles.

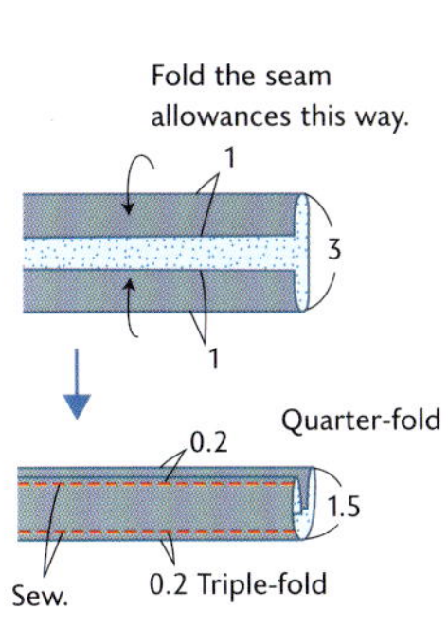

5. Sew together sides and bottom of exterior fabric.

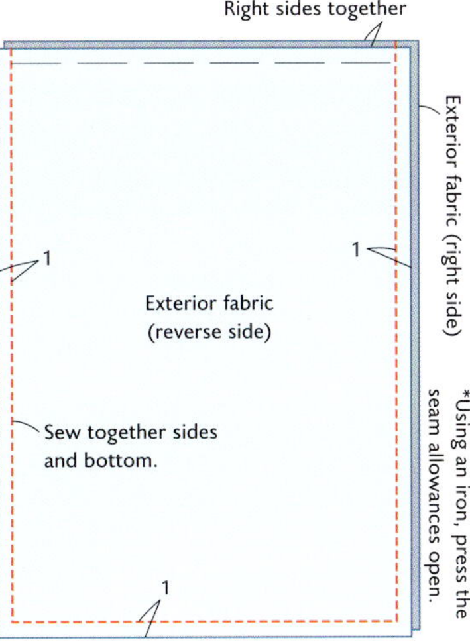

6. Sew together sides and bottom of lining fabric.

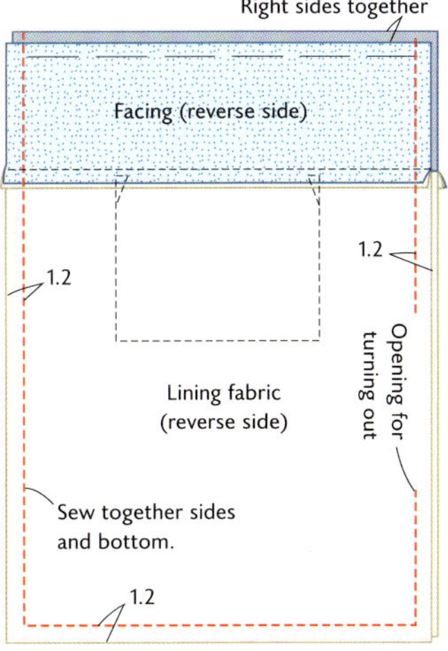

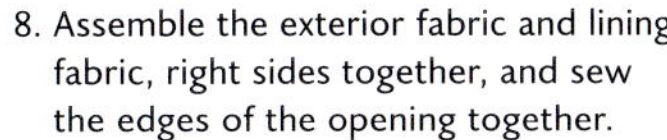

7. Baste handles.

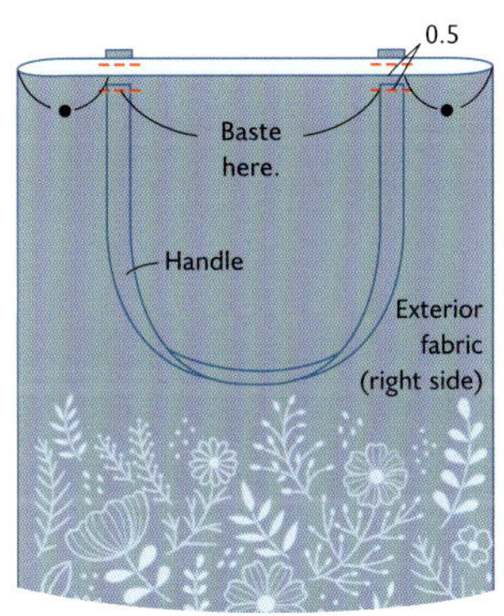

8. Assemble the exterior fabric and lining fabric, right sides together, and sew the edges of the opening together.

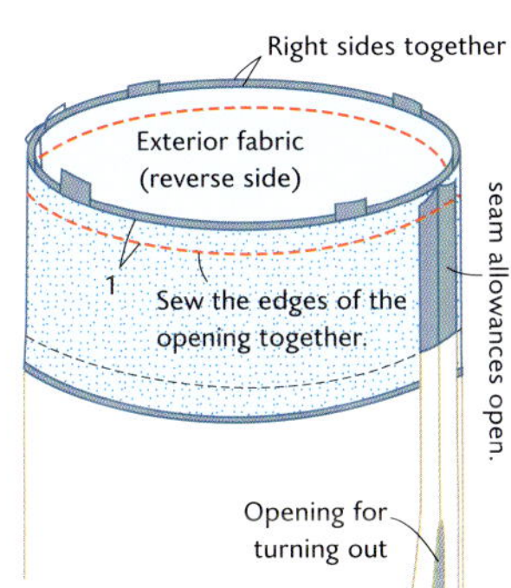

9. Turn the right side out and sew the opening closed.

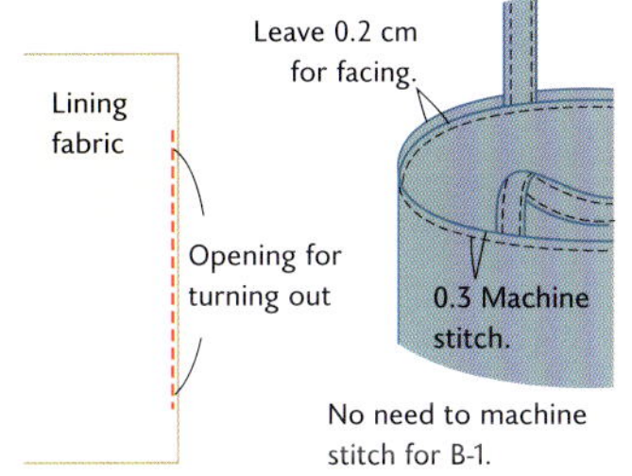

Finished project B-7

*If making a tablet case and not attaching handles . . .

Schematic *Follow the same instructions for the tote bag.

*Add 1-cm seam allowances.

Lining fabric (2 pieces)

Facing

5

5

Lining fabric

26.5

21.5

11.5 Opening for turning out

5

19.5

C Gusseted Pouches

Projects p. 14–15, 30–31 • Patterns p. 75–78

Finished measurements: 16 x 7 x 7 cm

Materials

No. 25 embroidery floss (colors listed on pattern pages)

Fabric Exterior fabric: Linen, 40 x 35 cm

Lining fabric: Cotton, 35 x 20 cm

Other: Cord, 90 cm

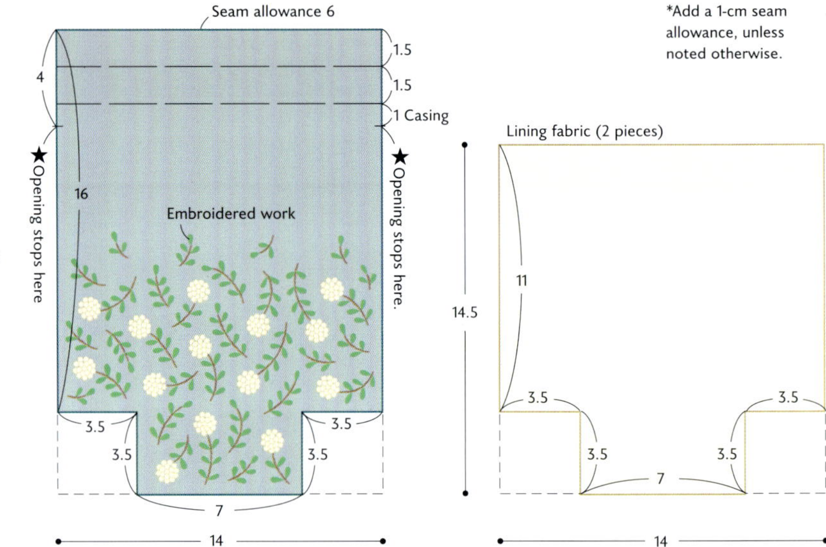

1. Work embroidery on the exterior fabric.

2. Cut fabric for each part, adding a 1-cm seam allowance all around.

3. Sew the exterior fabrics and lining fabrics together.

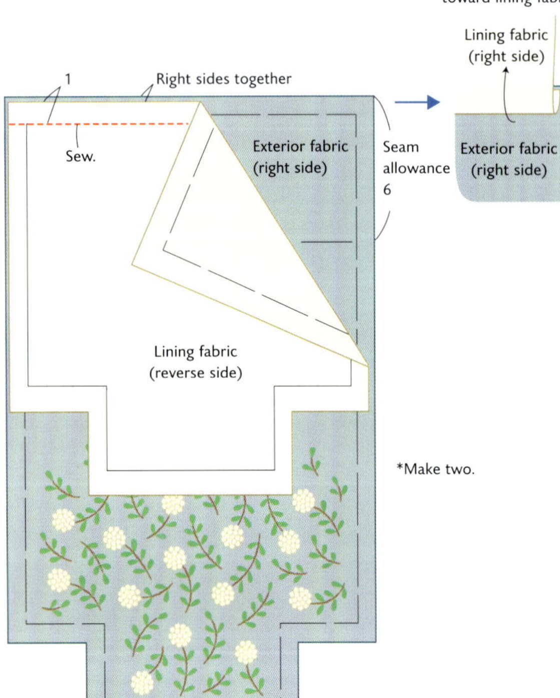

*Make two.

4. Assemble the two pieces, right sides together.

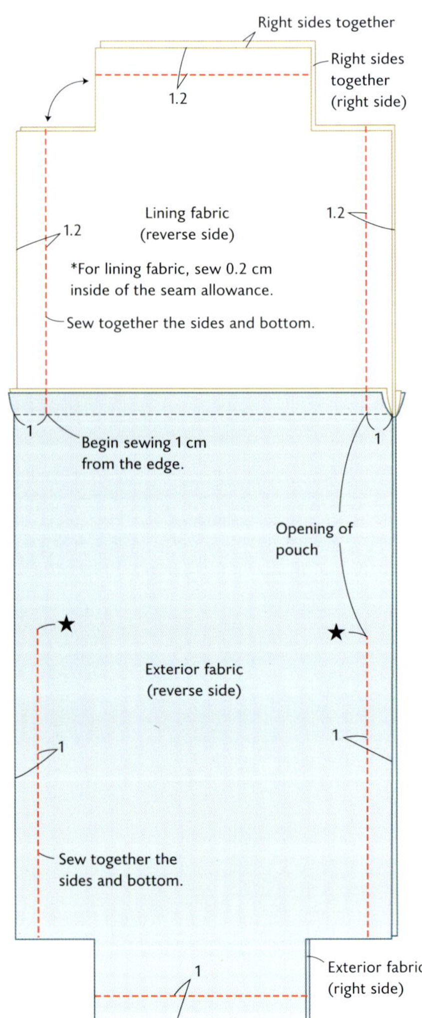

5. Sew gussets for the exterior fabric and lining fabric.

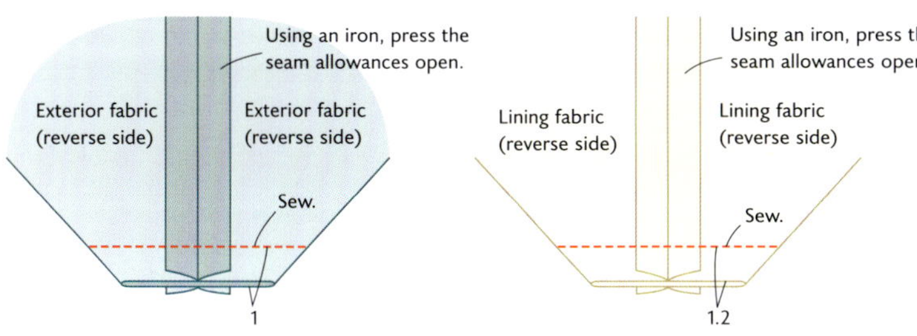

Fold the gusset's seam allowance toward the bottom.

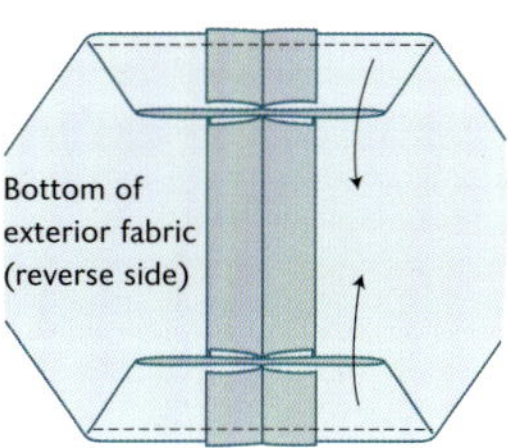

*Repeat for the lining fabric.

6. Sew the opening of the pouch.

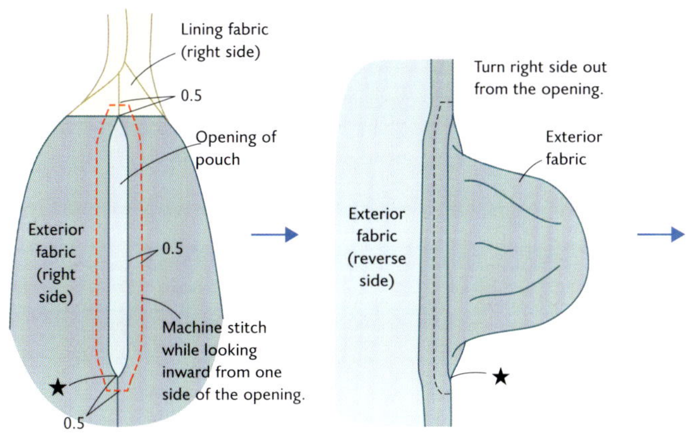

*Repeat for the other side of the opening.

7. Turn right side out.

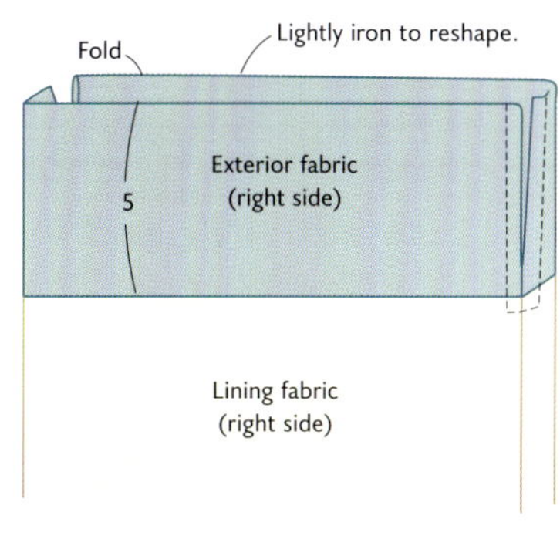

8. Make casings.

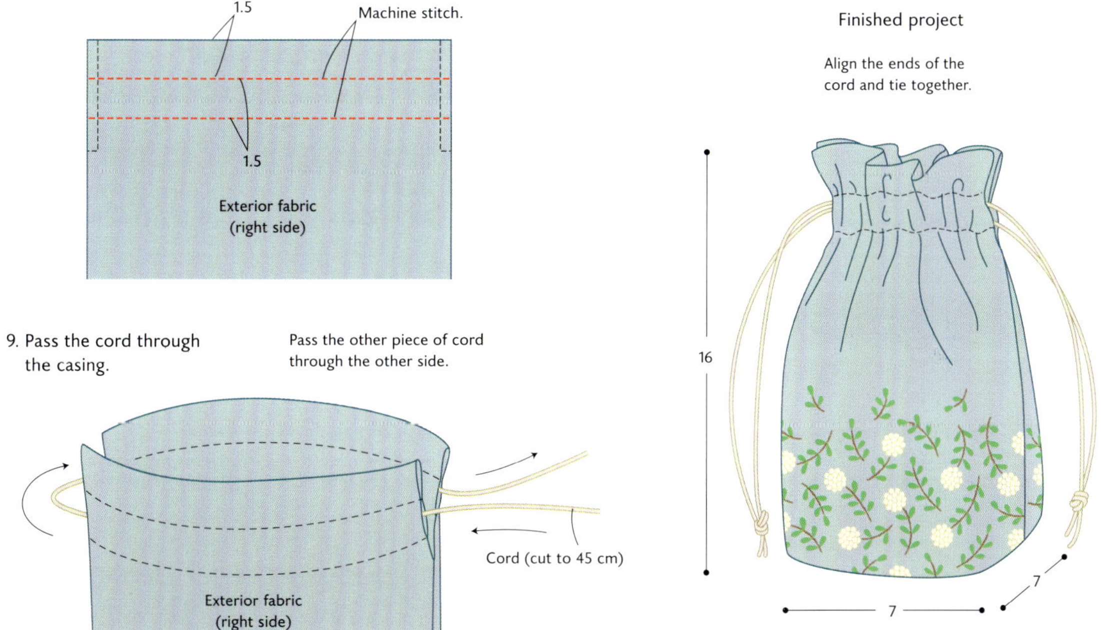

D Drawstring Pouches

Projects p. 16–17, 20, 31 • Patterns p. 79–83
Finished measurements: Refer to patterns (see p. 56 for pattern reading key)

Materials
No. 25 embroidery floss (colors listed on pattern pages)
Fabric

		Exterior fabric (linen)	Lining fabric (cotton)	Other (cord)
a	D-1, 2	40 x 35 cm	35 x 20 cm	90 cm
b	D-3	35 x 30 cm	30 x 15 cm	70 cm
c	D-4	40 x 35 cm	40 x 20 cm	90 cm
d	D-5	30 x 30 cm	30 x 15 cm	66 cm

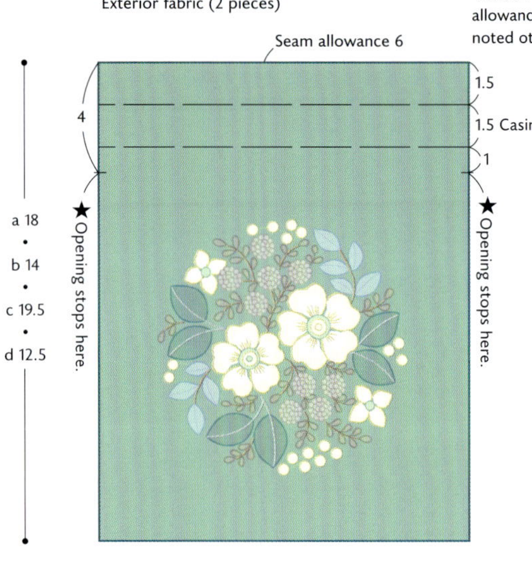

Lining fabric (2 pieces)

a 13 • b 9 • c 14.5 • d 7.5

a 14 • b 10 • c 14.5 • d 9

1. Work embroidery on the exterior fabric.

2. Cut the fabric for each part, adding a 1-cm seam allowance all around.

3. Sew the exterior fabrics and lining fabrics together.

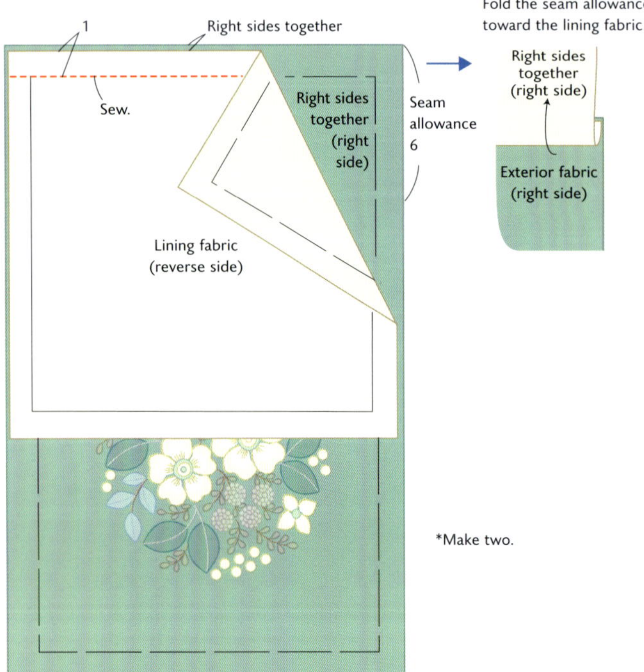

*Make two.

4. Assemble two pieces, right sides together.

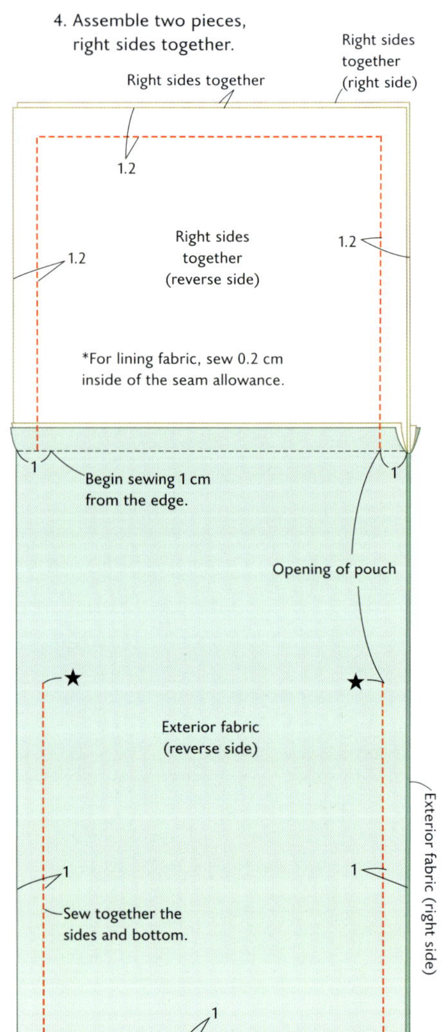

5. Sew the opening of the pouch.

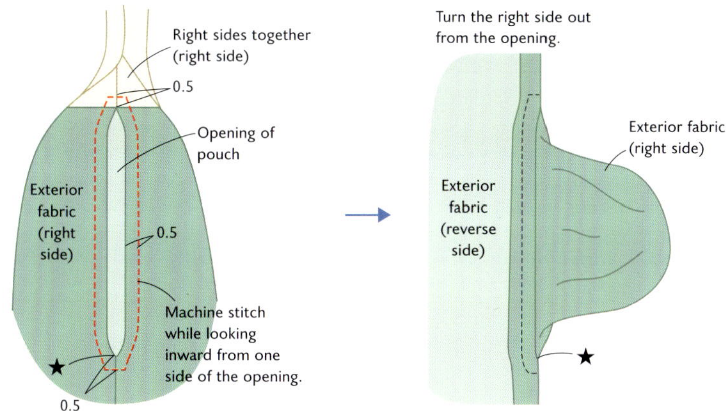

*Repeat for other side of opening.

6. Turn the right side out and make casings.

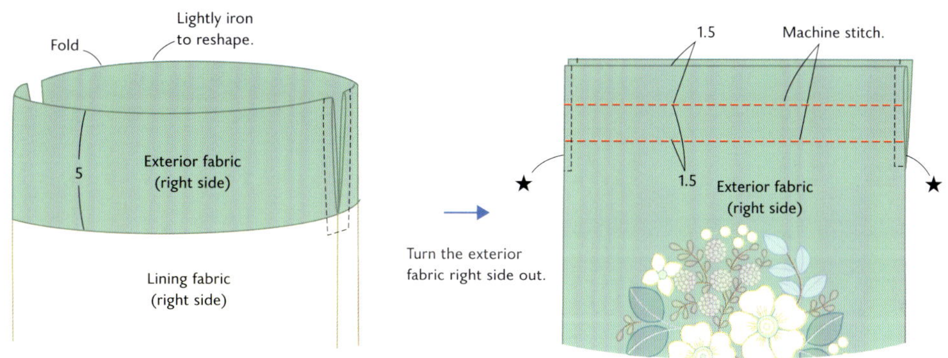

7. Pass the cord through the casing.

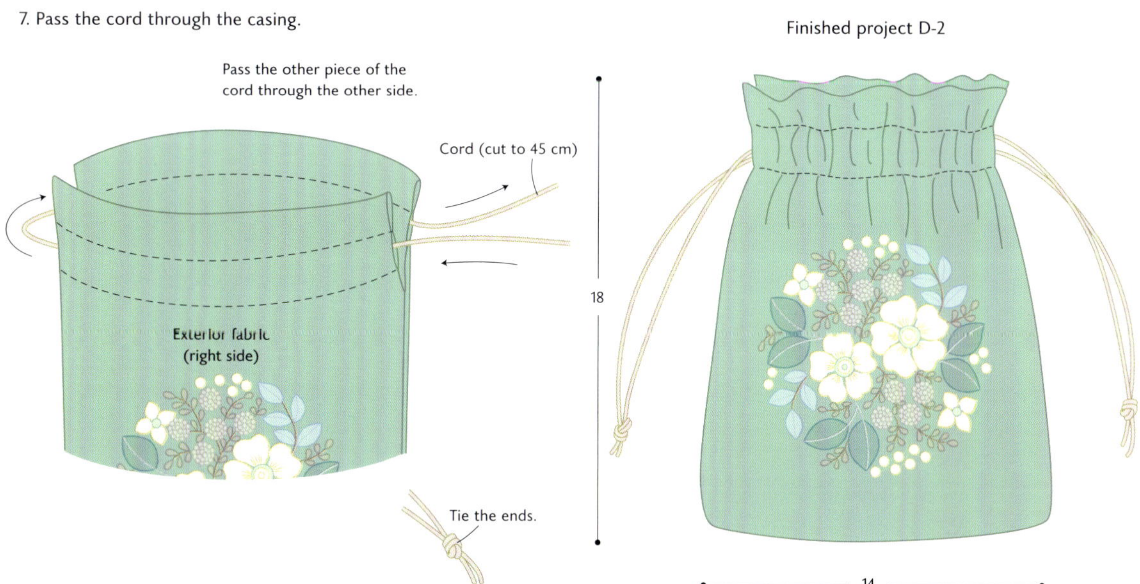

E Pincushions

Project p. 20 • Pattern p. 47
Finished measurements: Approximately 4.5 x 5.5 cm (see p. 56 for pattern reading key)

Materials
No. 25 embroidery floss (refer to the pattern)
Fabric Ground: Linen, 20 x 20 cm
Other: Fusible interfacing, 20 x 20 cm; wooden bowl, 1 piece (about a 6-cm diameter, 3 cm high); cotton wadding, as needed; glue
All embroidery floss is DMC No. 25; the number in parentheses is the number of strands.

E-a (blue)	1. 3760 (3)	7. 3841 (3)	13. 932 (2)
	2. 519 (3)	8. 930 (2)	14. 931 (2)
	3. 3841 (2)	9. 518 (2)	15. 3752 (2)
	4. 519 (2)	10. 3761 (2)	16. 930 (2)
	5. 3752 (2)	11. 3750 (2)	
	6. 3760 (2)	12. 931 (2)	
E-b (purple)	1. 3836 (3)	7. 3041 (3)	13. 3743 (2)
	2. 3042 (3)	8. 3743 (2)	14. 3740 (2)
	3. 3743 (2)	9. 3836 (2)	15. 3041 (2)
	4. 3042 (2)	10. 25 (2)	16. 3740 (2)
	5. 25 (2)	11. 3835 (2)	
	6. 3836 (2)	12. 3042 (2)	
E-c (green)	1. 987 (3)	7. 3364 (3)	13. 3052 (2)
	2. 3052 (3)	8. 524 (2)	14. 163 (2)
	3. 524 (2)	9. 3348 (2)	15. 471 (2)
	4. 989 (2)	10. 524 (2)	16. 3364 (2)
	5. 471 (2)	11. 561 (2)	
	6. 10 (2)	12. 3052 (2)	

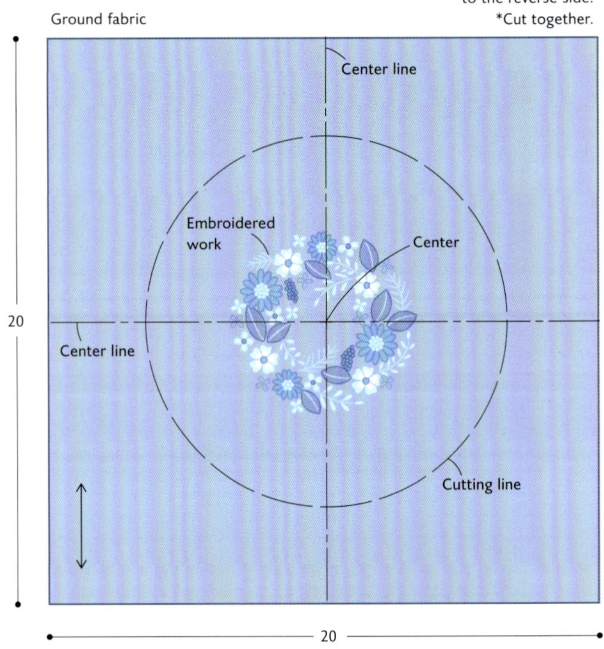

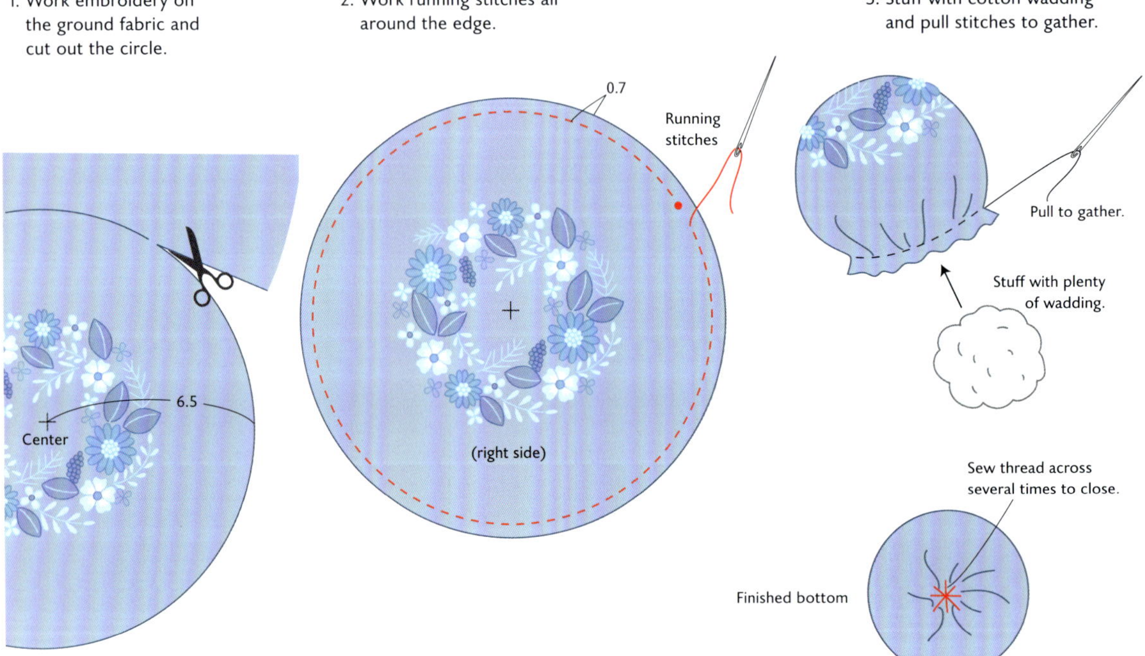

4. Insert into the wooden bowl.

Ground fabric (right side)

Insert the cushion into the bowl, making sure it's even, and secure it with glue. Press down lightly while waiting for it to dry. (You can also set it in place overnight with masking tape.)

Apply glue to the inside of the bowl.

Bowl

Finished project

Approximately 4.5

Approximately 5.5

Pattern (actual size)

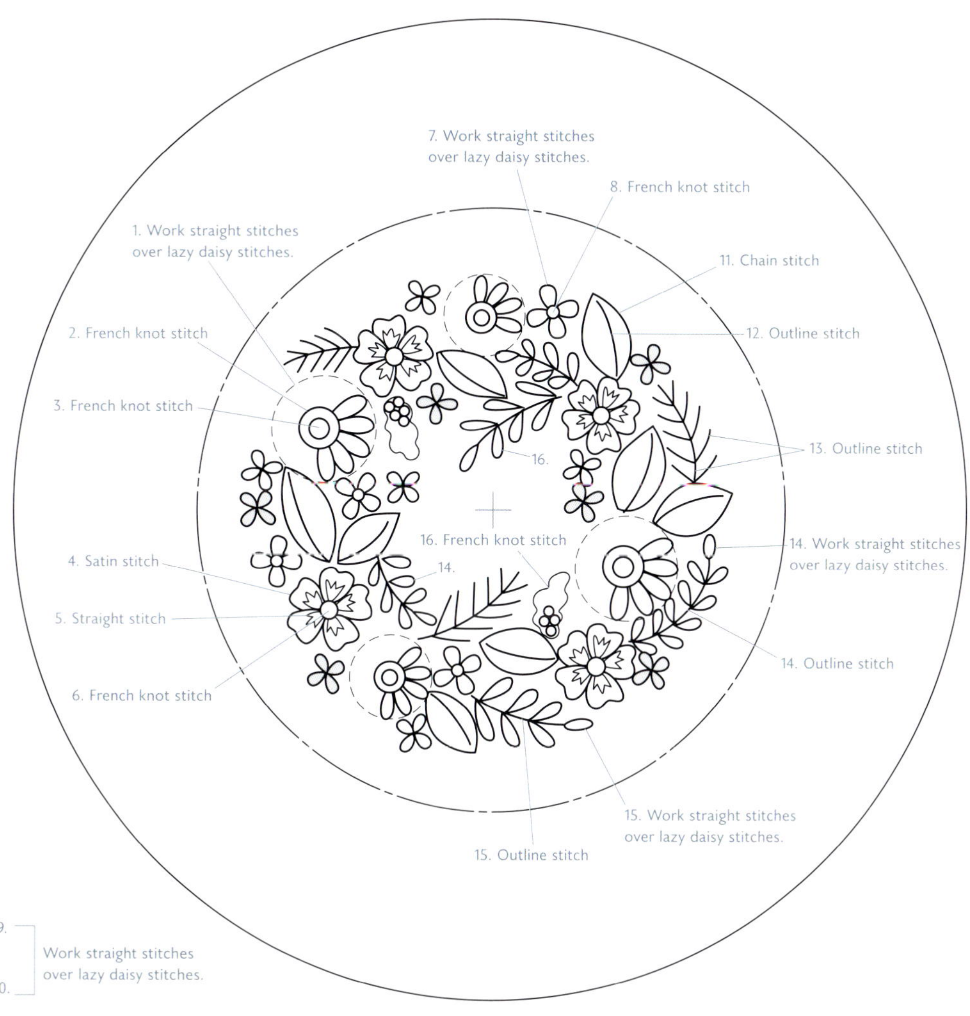

9.
10.
Work straight stitches over lazy daisy stitches.

F Fold-Over Trinket Pouch

Project p. 21 • Pattern p. 49
Finished measurements: 7 x 6.5 cm (see p. 56 for pattern reading key)

Materials
No. 25 embroidery floss (refer to pattern)
Fabric Main fabric: Linen, 30 x 30 cm
Other: 0.8-cm-diameter snaps, 2 pieces; stay tape, 20 cm
All embroidery floss is DMC No. 25; the number in parentheses is the number of strands.

F-a (yellow)	1. 746 (2)	4. 746 (2)	7. 745 (2)
	2. 3823 (2)	5. 744 (3)	8. 10 (2)
	3. 3823 (3)	6. 3823 (2)	9. 744 (3)
F-b (blue)	1. 3865 (2)	4. 5979 (2)	7. 597 (2)
	2. 598 (2)	5. 3810 (3)	8. 828 (2)
	3. 598 (3)	6. 828 (2)	9. 828 (3)
F-c (pink)	1. 23 (2)	4. 23 (2)	7. 3833 (2)
	2. 3713 (2)	5. 760 (3)	8. 3713 (2)
	3. 3326 (3)	6. 761 (2)	9. 761 (3)

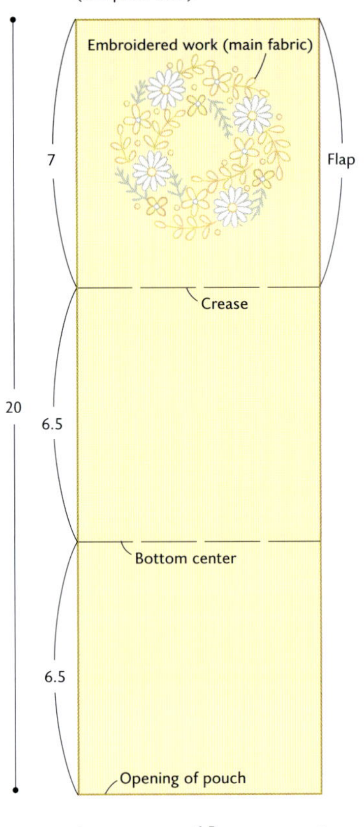

1. Work embroidery on the main fabric.

2. Cut fabric for the main fabric and inner lining, adding a 1-cm seam allowance all around.

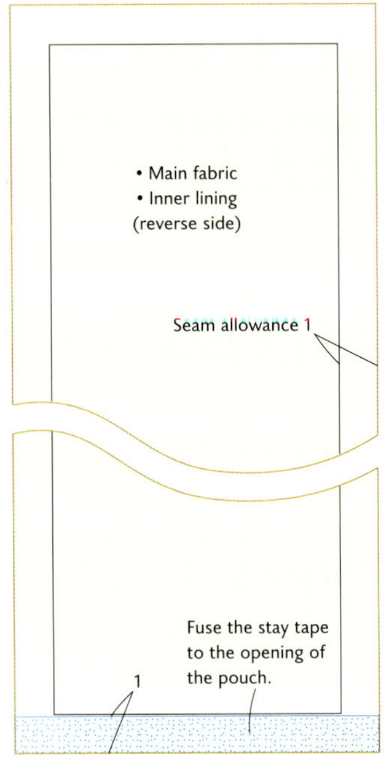

3. Sew sides.

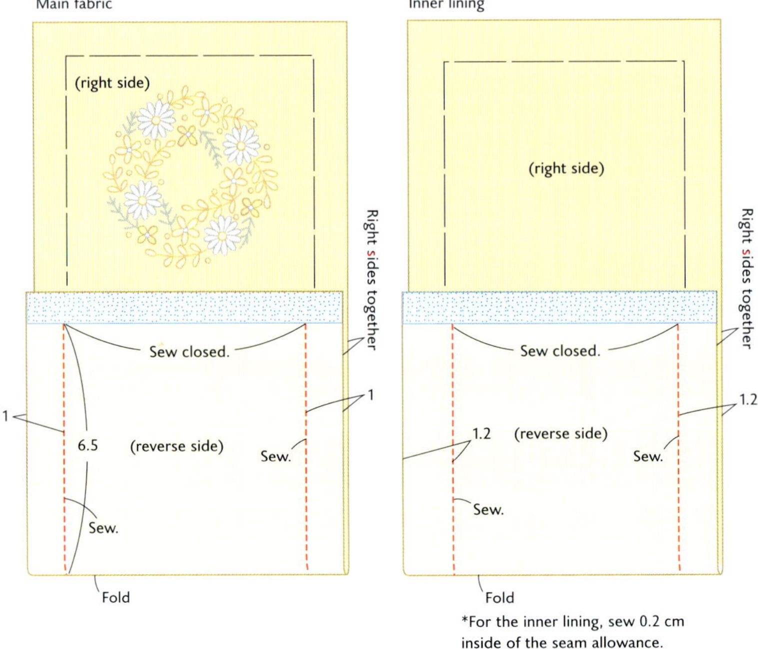

4. Sew the flaps.

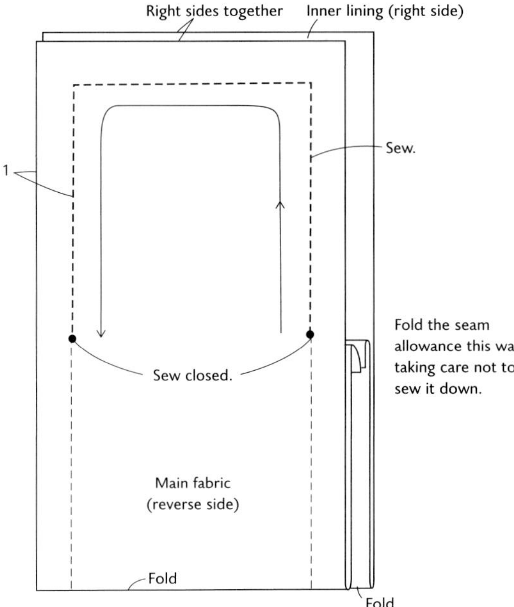

5. Turn right side out.

(1) Turn the flap right side out.

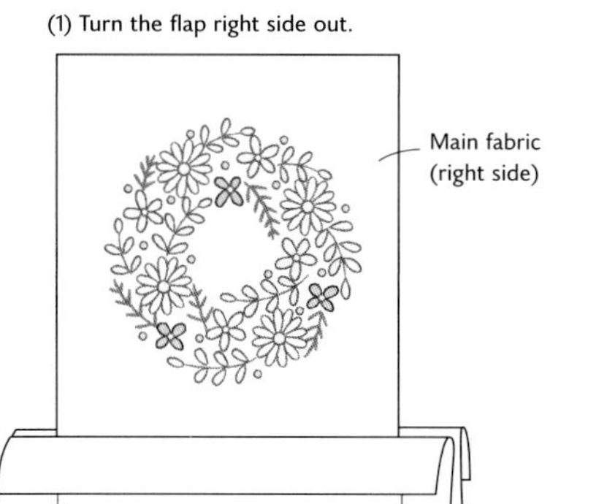

Fold the seam allowance inward, wrapping it with the pouch of the inner lining.

Main fabric (reverse side)

(2) Turn the pouch right side out.
(3) Lightly iron to reshape.

6. Close the opening of the pouch.

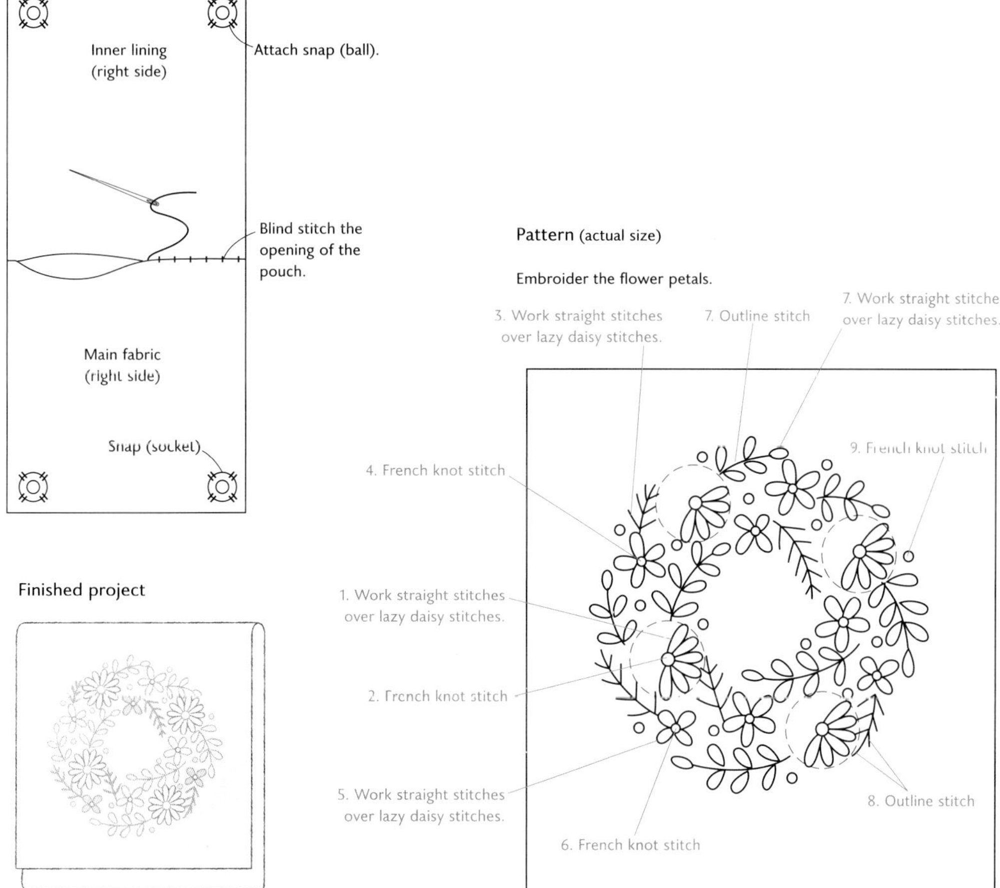

G Glasses Case

Project p. 22, 32 • Pattern pp. 84–86
Finished measurements: 6.5 x 16 cm

Materials
No. 25 embroidery floss (colors listed on pattern pages)
Fabric Exterior fabric: Linen, 30 x 30 cm
Lining fabric: Cotton, 20 x 20 cm
Other: Fusible quilt batting, 30 x 30 cm

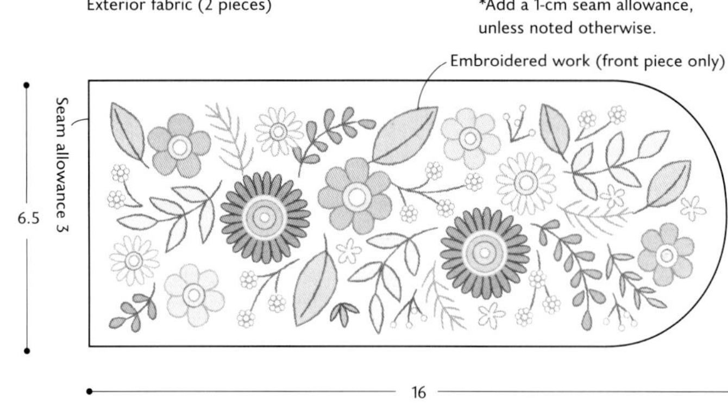

1. Work embroidery on the exterior fabric.

2. Cut the fabric for each part, adding a 1-cm seam allowance all around.

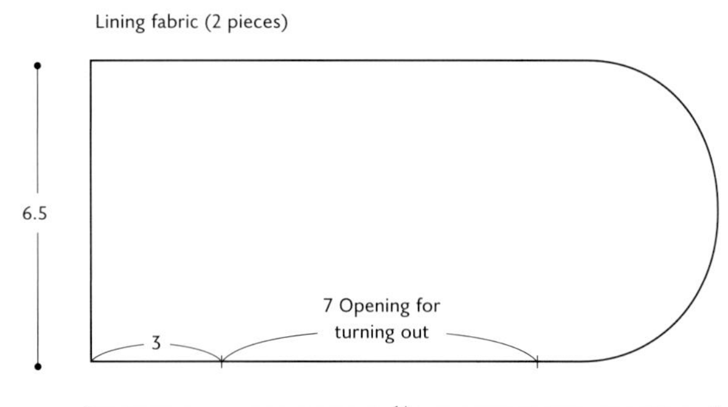

3. Attach the fusible quilt batting to the exterior fabric.

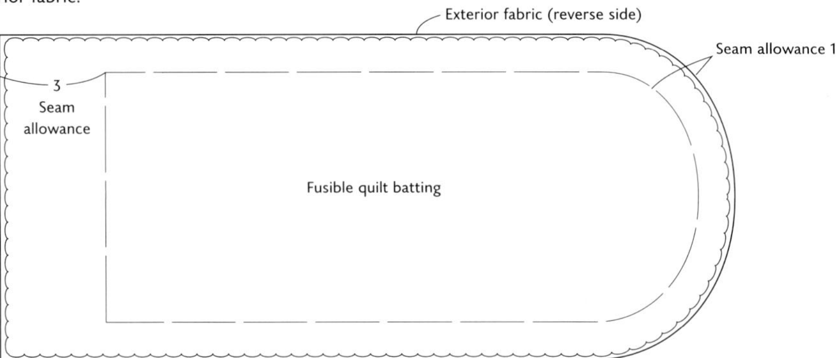

4. Sew together the exterior fabric and lining fabric.

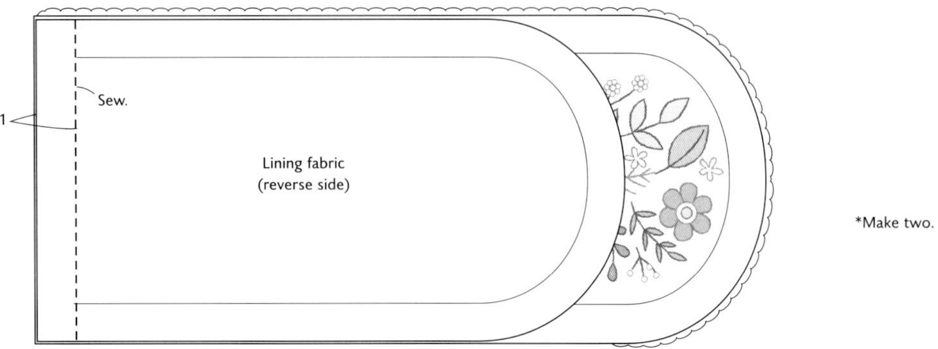

*Make two.

5. Assemble two pieces, right sides together.

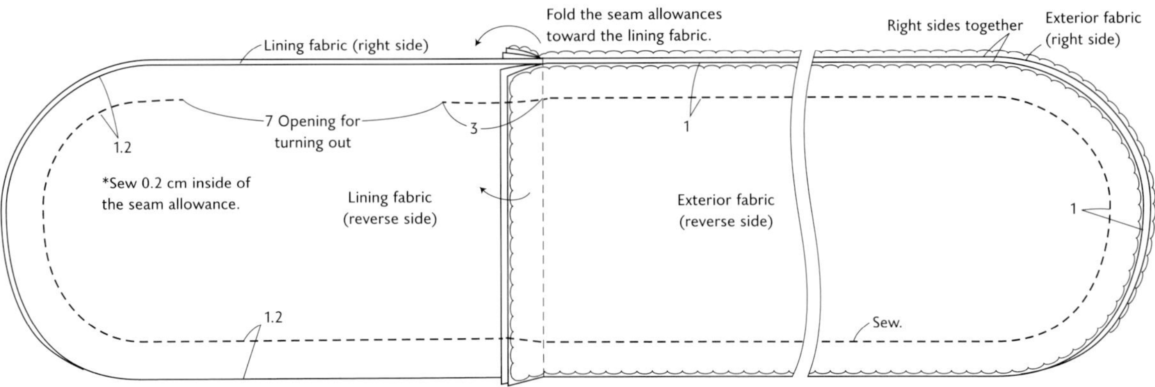

6. Turn right side out and close the opening for turning out.

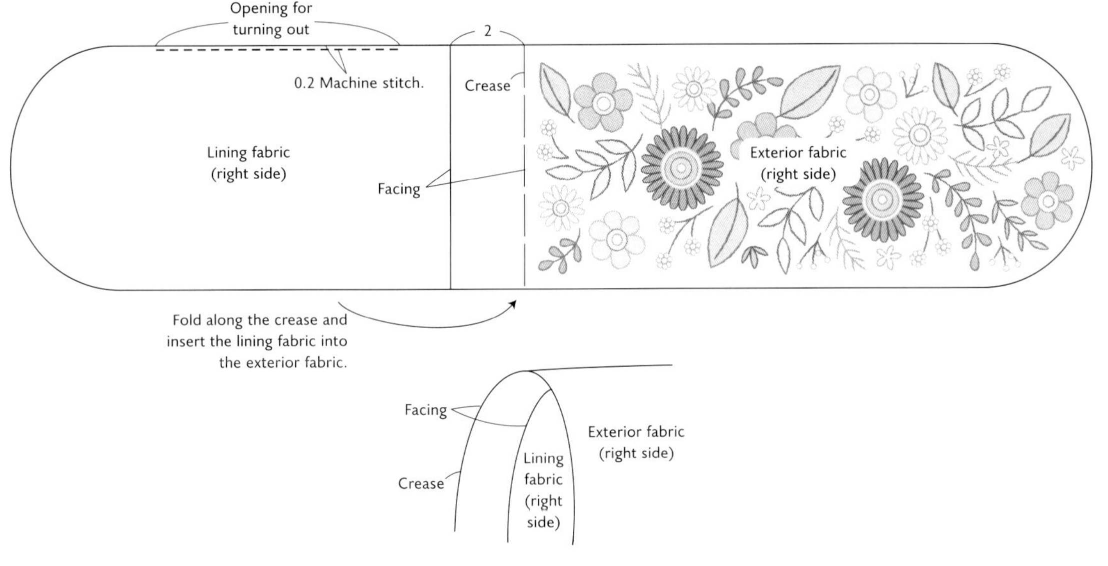

Finished project

H Pen Case

Project p. 22, 32 • Pattern pp. 84–86
Finished measurements: 6.5 x 17 cm

Materials
No. 25 embroidery floss (refer to pattern)
Fabric Exterior fabric: Linen, 25 x 25 cm
Lining fabric: Cotton, 25 x 25 cm
Other: 16-cm-long zipper, 1 piece; stay tape, 40 cm

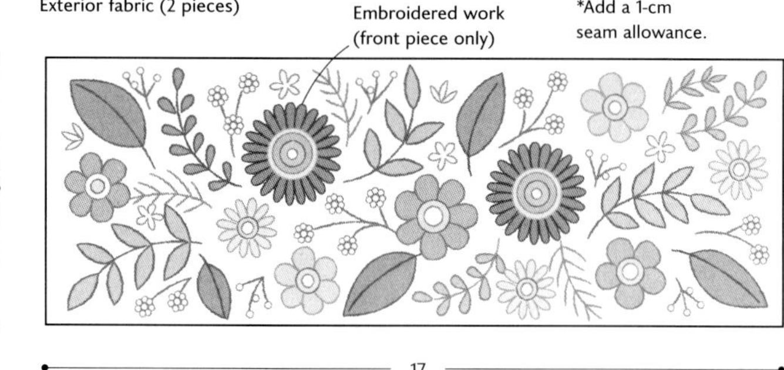

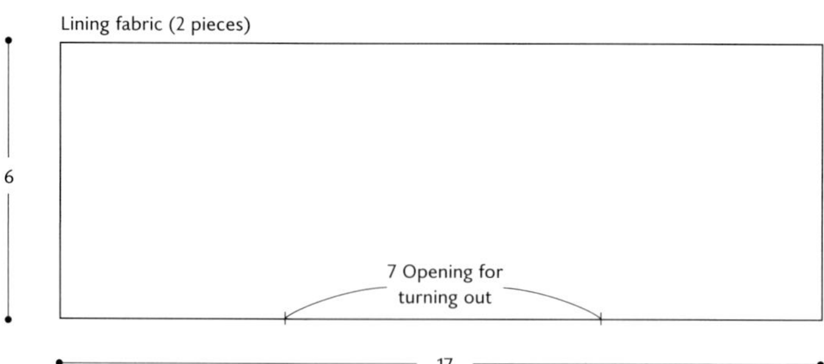

1. Work embroidery on the exterior fabric.
2. Cut the fabric for each part, adding a 1-cm seam allowance all around.
3. Attach a zipper to the exterior fabric and lining fabric.

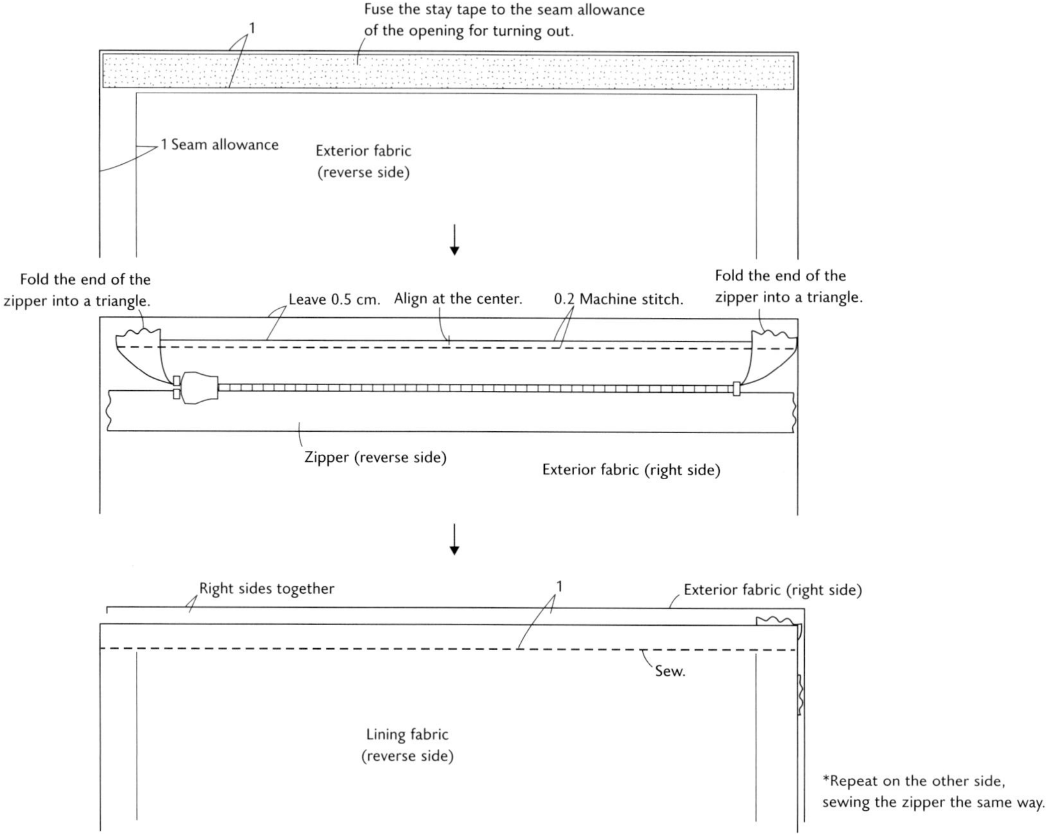

*Repeat on the other side, sewing the zipper the same way.

4. Assemble each set of exterior and lining fabrics, right sides together.

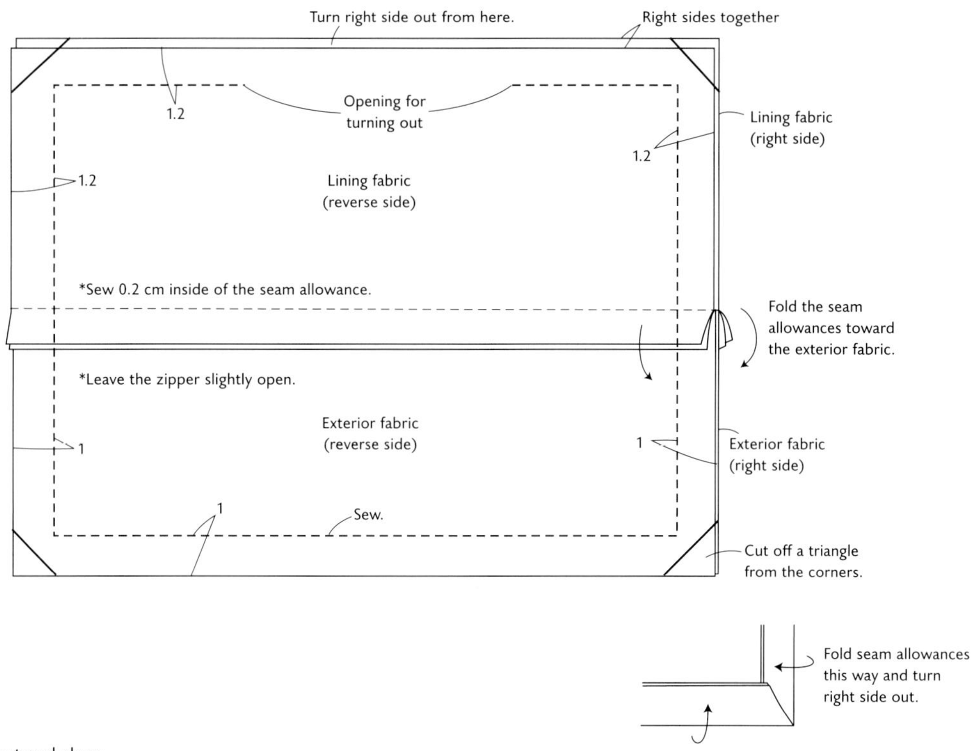

5. Turn right side out and close the opening for turning out.

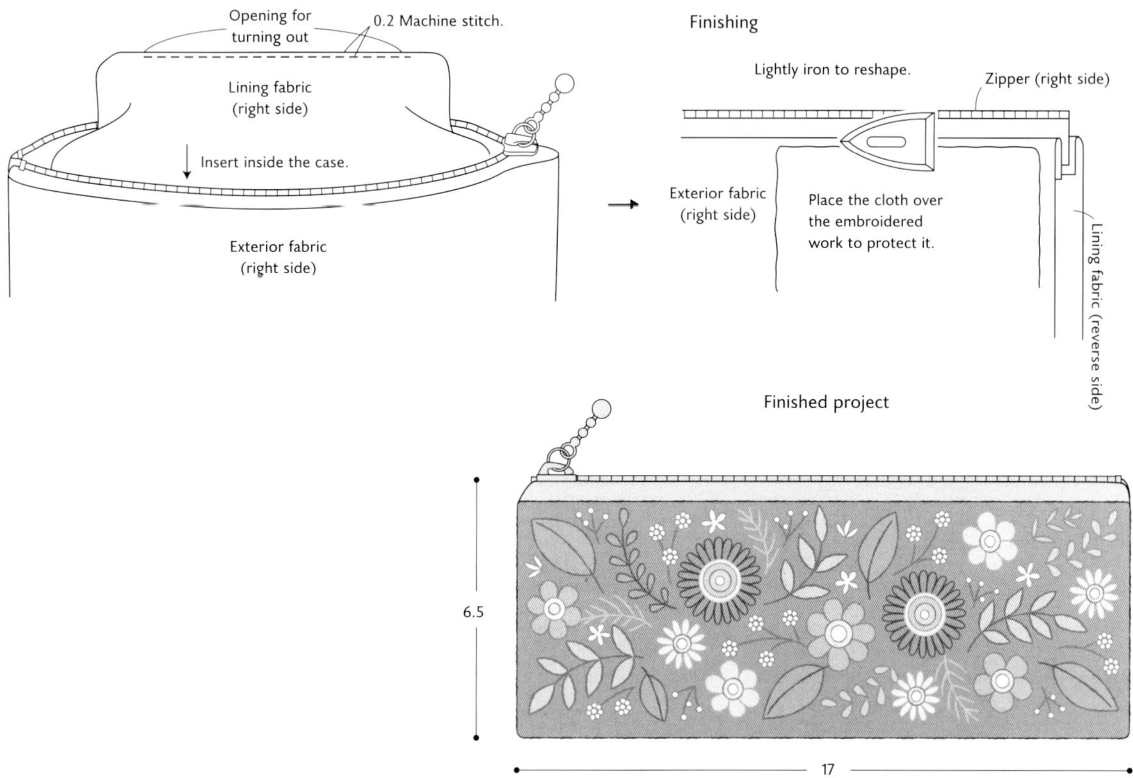

I Brooches

Project pp. 24–25 • Pattern pp. 55, 87
Finished measurements: 3.5-cm diameter (see p. 56 for pattern reading key)

Materials (for each piece)
No. 25 embroidery floss (refer to pattern)
Fabric Front & back side: Linen, 20 x 15 cm
Other: Fusible interfacing, 20 x 15 cm; 3.5-cm-diameter plastic button, 1 piece; cardboard, 4 x 4 cm; craft brooch pin, 1 piece

I-1a, b, c Nuance

All embroidery floss is DMC No. 25; the number in parentheses is the number of strands.

I-1a (beige)	1. ECRU (3)	2. 3864 (3)	3. 842 (2)
I-1b (pale green)	1. 10 (3)	2. 3348 (3)	3. 3348 (2)
I-1c (lavender)	1. 27 (3)	2. 25 (3)	3. 26 (2)

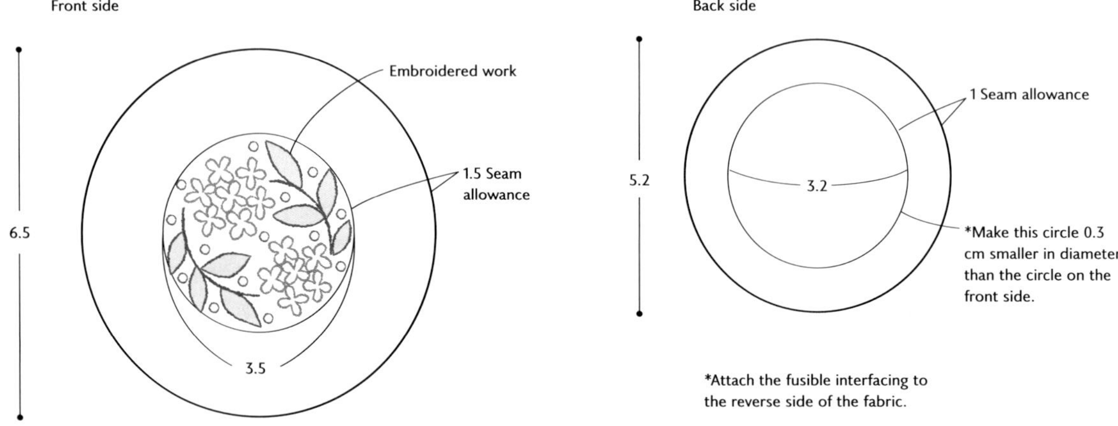

1. Work embroidery on the front side of the fabric.
2. Cut fabric for the front side and back side, adding a 1-cm seam allowance all around.
3. Make the front side.

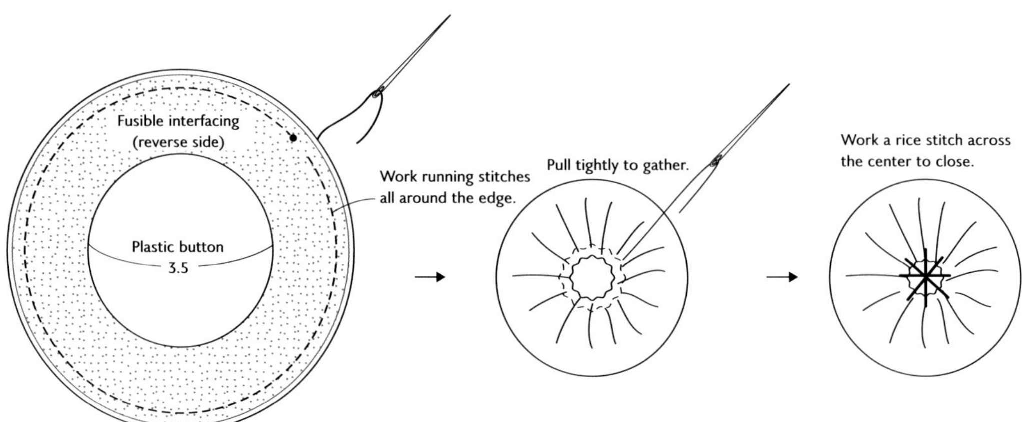

4. Make the back side.

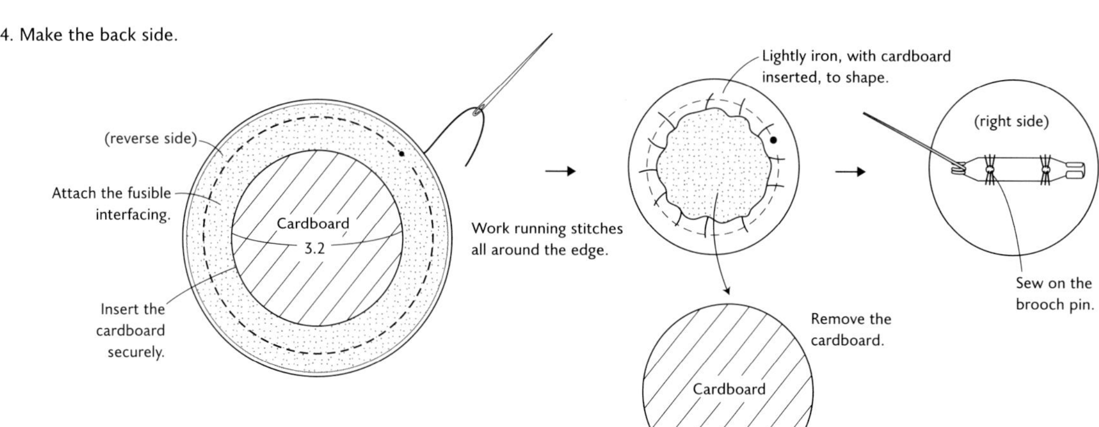

5. Sew together the front side and back side.

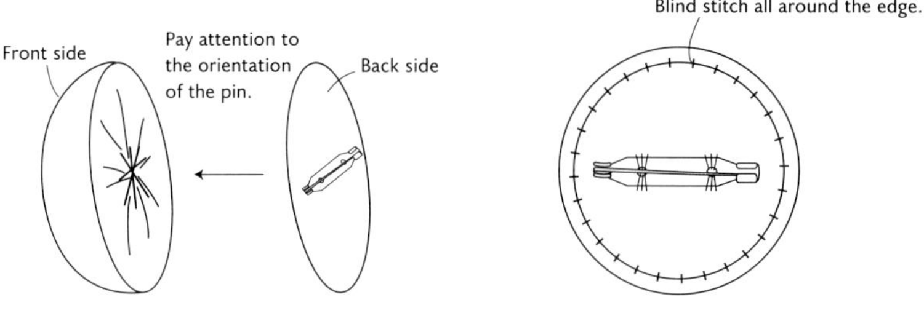

Finished project

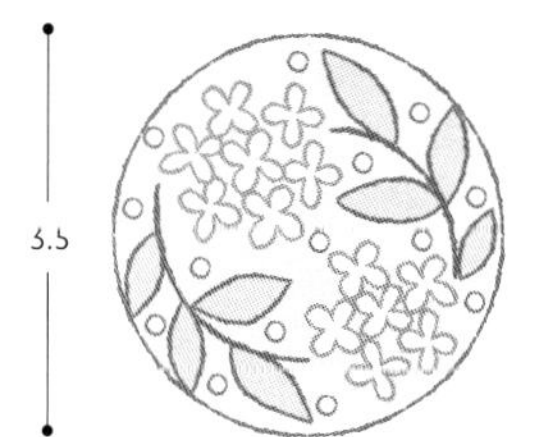

Pattern (actual size)

11a, b, c Nuance

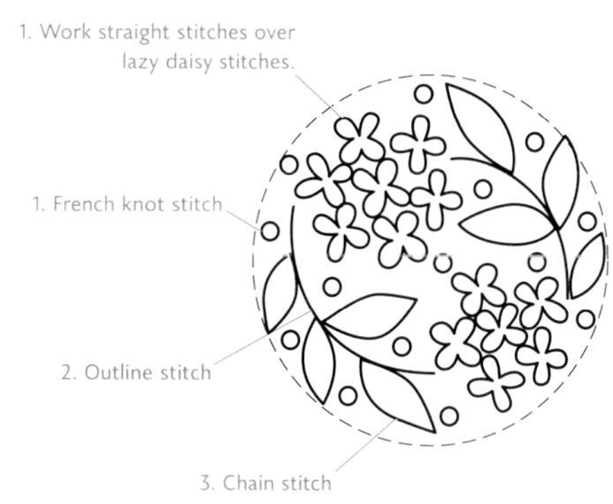

PATTERNS

How to Read the Patterns

The pattern pages show only the embroidery instructions.
Please see pages 39–55 for instructions on how to make each item.

HOW TO READ THE PROJECT NUMBERS, CODES, AND SYMBOLS

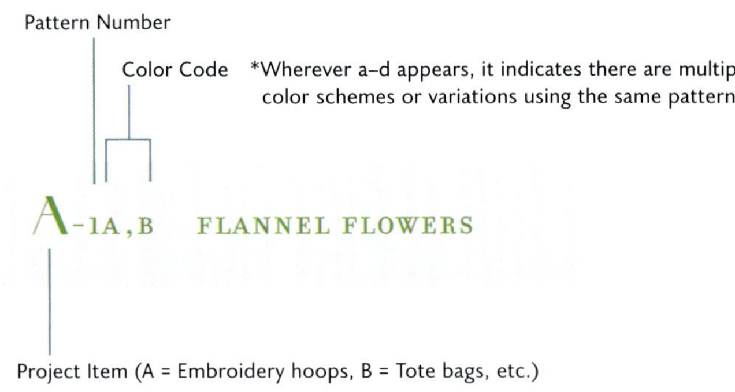

WHEN THERE ARE MULTIPLE COLOR SCHEMES OR VARIATIONS

In these cases, the pattern and stitches are the same, but the color of the embroidery floss is different. Check the charts for each version carefully. Each number is followed by the color code for the embroidery floss, and the number in parentheses indicates the number of strands. These correspond with the numbers that appear in the pattern itself before the name of the stitches.

HOW TO READ THE PATTERNS

Each pattern includes a variety of stitches. For patterns where there is only one color option, the color codes for the embroidery floss and the number of strands are indicated on the pattern itself.

FABRICS USED IN THIS BOOK

There are many fabrics that can be used for needlework, but most of the embroidery patterns in this book call for plain-weave linen. I recommend using linen or cotton that has a fine texture. Linen is especially pliable, so it's less likely to be straining on your fingers while stitching. Although I don't recommend using linen that's too thin and flimsy, it's important to find linen that's a comfortable weight for your fingers.

FUSIBLE INTERFACING

For projects that you hope to use in your daily life or have around for a long time, it's helpful to add fusible interfacing to the reverse side of your ground fabric as a lining. Since shrinking or puckering can occur with linen after fusing the interfacing and working in the embroidery, it's best to add an extra 5–10 cm of linen to the finished measurements and then, once you've completed the embroidery, trim the excess fabric.

A-1a, b FLANNEL FLOWERS

Project pp. 6, 27 • Actual size

All embroidery floss is DMC No. 25; the number in parentheses is the number of strands.

A-1a (khaki)			
	1. ECRU (2)	4. 644 (2) + 3023 (1)	7. 3052
	2. 3013 (2)	5. 3022 (2) + 3023 (1)	8. 644 (2)
	3. 10 (2)	6. 3348 (2)	9. 3364 (2) + 644 (1)

A-1b (white)			
	1. 775 (2)	4. 3753 (2) + 3325 (1)	7. 3325 (2)
	2. 3755 (2)	5. 825 (2) + 3325 (1)	8. 3753 (1) + 3325 (1)
	3. 3325 (2)	6. 334 (2)	9. 826 (2) + 3325 (1)

3. Straight stitch
4. French knot stitch
1. Satin stitch
2. Satin stitch
5. French knot stitch
6. Satin stitch
7. Satin stitch
8. French knot stitch
9. Chain stitch

A-2 MIMOSAS

Project p. 7 • Actual size

All embroidery floss is FUJIX, either Soie et or MOCO.

For stitches using Soie et, use 3 strands unless noted otherwise, and wrap French knot stitches 2 times. For stitches using MOCO, use 1 strand unless noted otherwise, and wrap French knot stitches 3 times.

Straight stitch Soie et 620 (2)
Outline stitch Soie et 620

A-3 BLUE DAISIES

Project p. 8 • Actual size

All embroidery floss is DMC No. 25; the number in parentheses is the number of strands.

A-5A, B FLORET WREATH

Project pp. 8, 27 • Actual size

All embroidery floss is DMC No. 25; the number in parentheses is the number of strands.

A-5a (green)	1. 502 (2)	5. 3817 (3)	9. –	13. 319 (2)
	2. 3024 (1)	6. 500 (2)	10. 501 (2)	14. 503 (2)
	3. 163 (3)	7. 501 (3)	11. 502 (2)	15. 520 (3)
	4. 163 (4)	8. 501 (2)	12. 319 (4)	16. 520 (2)

A-5b (black)	1. ECRU (2)	5. ECRU (3)	9. ECRU (1)	13. ECRU (2)
	2. –	6. ECRU (2)	10. ECRU (2)	14. ECRU (2)
	3. ECRU (3)	7. ECRU (3)	11. ECRU (2)	15. ECRU (3)
	4. ECRU (4)	8. ECRU (2)	12. ECRU (4)	16. ECRU (2)

A-4A, B FLOWERS ON THE BREEZE

Project pp. 8, 27 • Actual size

All embroidery floss is DMC No. 25; the number in parentheses is the number of strands.

A-4a (green)	1. 3865 (2)	9. 3822 (2)	17. 502 (3)	25. 3064 (3)
	2. 10 (2)	10. 677 (4)	18. 561 (2)	26. 841 (3)
	3. 472 (2)	11. 746 (3)	19. 3863 (3)	27. 24 (3)
	4. 10 (4)	12. ECRU (2)	20. 3863 (2)	28. 3348 (3)
	5. 712 (3)	13. 745 (2)	21. 367 (2)	29. 3348 (2)
	6. 10 (2)	14. 3346 (3)	22. 840 (3)	30. 3753 (5)
	7. 712 (2)	15. 3346 (2)	23. 471 (2)	31. 3013 (3)
	8. 677 (2)	16. 3072 (3)	24. 801 (3)	

A-4b (pink)	1. 3328 (2)	9. 3865 (2)	17. 471 (3)	25. 712 (3)
	2. 760 (2)	10. 739 (4)	18. 987 (2)	26. 3864 (3)
	3. 353 (2)	11. ECRU (3)	19. 3863 (3)	27. 746 (3)
	4. 10 (4)	12. 3865 (2)	20. 3863 (2)	28. 3348 (3)
	5. 746 (3)	13. 745 (2)	21. 561 (2)	29. 3348 (2)
	6. 10 (2)	14. 988 (3)	22. 3862 (3)	30. 760 (5)
	7. 353 (2)	15. 988 (2)	23. 471 (2)	31. 3052 (3)
	8. 3770 (2)	16. 819 (3)	24. 801 (3)	

A-6 MARGUERITE WREATH

Project p. 9 • Actual size

All embroidery floss is DMC No. 25; the number in parentheses is the number of strands.

A-7A, B LEAF WREATH

Project p. 27 • Actual size

All embroidery floss is DMC No. 25; the number in parentheses is the number of strands.

A-7a (black)	1. 3866 (4)	4. 3866 (2)
	2. 648 (4)	5. 648 (2)
	3. 645 (4)	6. 645 (2)

A-7b (white)	1. 745 (3) + 746 (1)	4. 745 (1) + 746 (1)
	2. 165 (3) + 746 (1)	5. 165 (1) + 746 (1)
	3. 165 (2) + 989 (2)	6. 165 (1) + 989 (1)

For 1–3, work straight stitches over lazy daisy stitches.
For 4–6, work outline stitches.

1
4
5
2
6
3

B-1 HEALING FLOWERS

Project p. 11 • Actual size

All embroidery floss is DMC No. 25; the number in parentheses is the number of strands.

B-2 A WALK IN THE FOREST

Project p. 11 • Actual size

All embroidery floss is DMC No. 25; the number in parentheses is the number of strands.

B-4A, B, C, D GARDEN PARTY

Project pp. 13, 29 • Actual size

All embroidery floss is DMC No. 25.

B-4a (deep navy)	644
B-4b (moss green)	648

B-4c (light brown)	453
B-4b (mustard yellow)	822

Work chain stitch (2) unless noted otherwise.
Fill in the shaded portions using chain stitch.

B-3 A POSY OF MARGUERITES

Project p. 12 • Actual size

All embroidery floss is DMC No. 25; the number in parentheses is the number of strands.

B-5a, b FIELD OF TREES

Project p. 28 • Actual size

All embroidery floss is DMC No. 25; the number in parentheses is the number of strands.

*Unless noted otherwise, use ECRU (2 strands) for 5a and 561 (2 strands) for 5b.

B-5a (khaki)			
	1. 3782 (2)	4. 3782 (2)	7. ECRU (3)
	2. ECRU (1)	5. 3782 (2)	8. 3782 (2)
	3. ECRU (3)	6. 3782 (4)	

B-5b (beige)			
	1. 801 (2)	4. 3863 (2)	7. 10 (3)
	2. 561 (1)	5. 987 (2)	8. 989 (2)
	3. 3822 (3)	6. 987 (4)	9. 3348 (2)

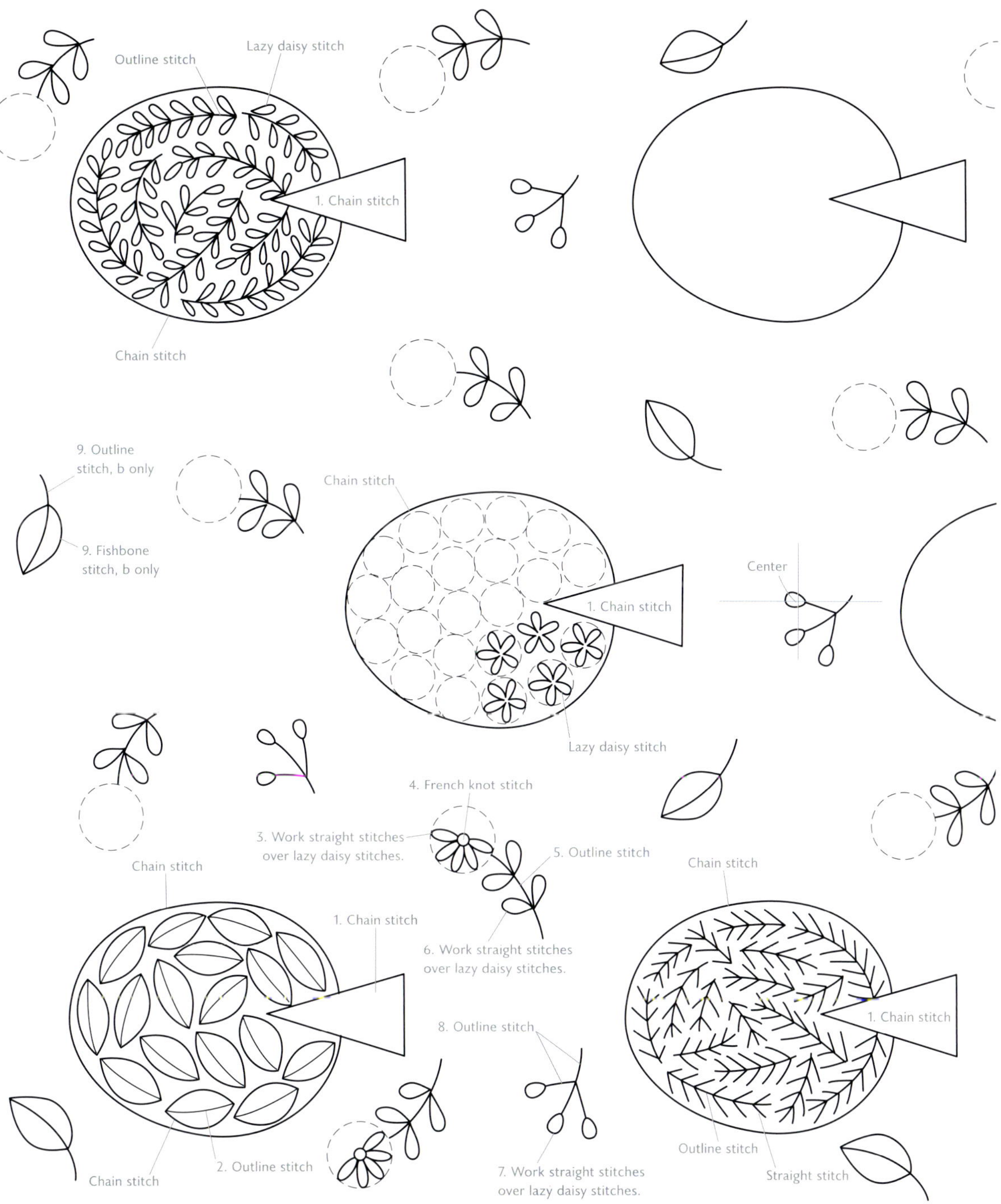

B-6A, B MARGUERITES

Project p. 28 • Enlarge pattern by 140%.

All embroidery floss is DMC No. 25; the number in parentheses is the number of strands.

B-6a (pink)	1. 3865 (3)	3. 3364 (2)	B-6b (yellow)	1. 3865 (3)	3. 989 (2)
	2. 745 (2)	4. 3865 (2)		2. 745 (2)	4. 3865 (2)

B-7 FIELD OF FLOWERS

Project p. 29 • Enlarge pattern by 120%.

All stitches are worked with DMC No. 25 3023 in chain stitch (2 strands) unless noted otherwise by the number in parentheses.

Fill in shaded portions using chain stitch (2).

B-8 PARADISE

Project p. 29 • Enlarge pattern by 120%.

All embroidery floss is DMC No. 25; the number in parentheses is the number of strands.

C-1A, B, C, D FOREST

Project pp. 14, 30 • Actual size

All embroidery floss is DMC No. 25. Work all stitches in one color; the number in parentheses is the number of strands.

Work in chain stitch (2 strands) unless noted otherwise.

C-1a (moss green)	ECRU
C-1b (brown)	644
C-1c (black)	648
C-1d (mustard yellow)	712

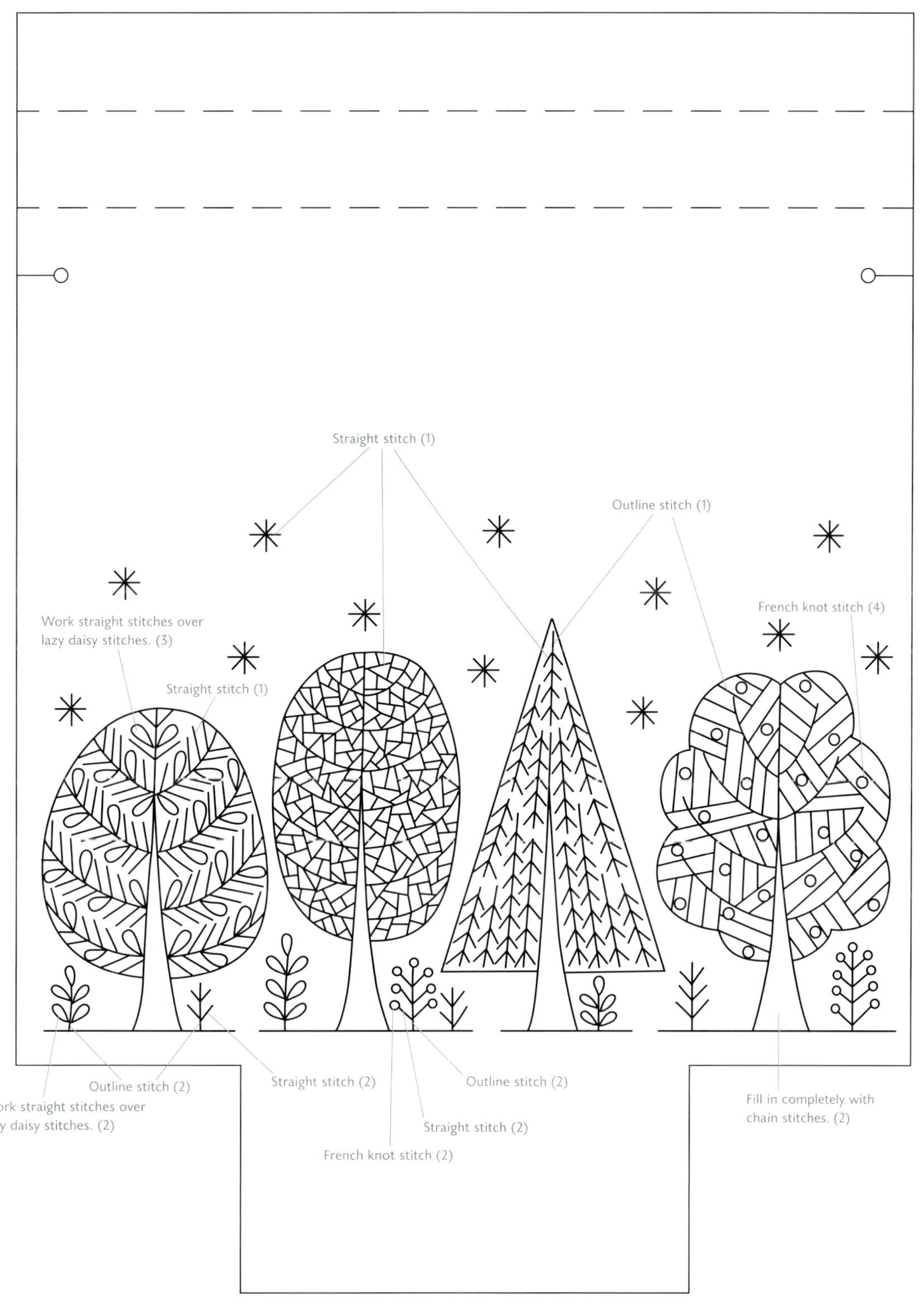

C-2A, B, C, D GENTLE BREEZE

Project pp. 14, 30 • Actual size

All embroidery floss is DMC No. 25; the number in parentheses is the number of strands.

C-2a (blue-gray)	1. ECRU (4)	C-2c (mustard yellow)	1. 822 (4)
	2. 987 (3)		2. 3011 (3)
	3. 3781 (2)		3. 839 (2)
C-2b (khaki)	1. 3045 (4)	C-2d (brown)	1. 816 (4)
	2. 3787 (3)		2. 520 (3)
	3. 640 (2)		3. 779 (2)

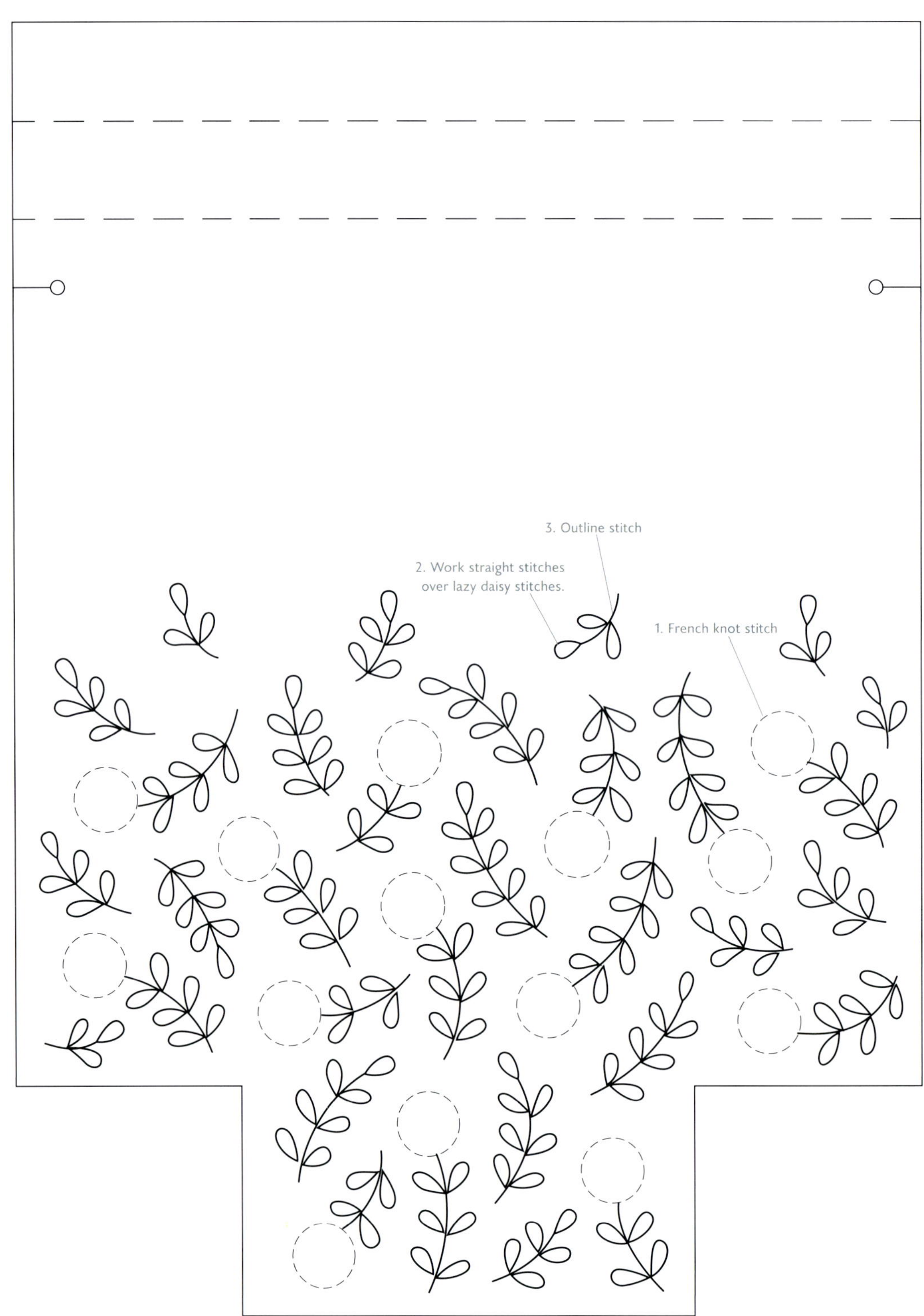

C-3A, B, C, D WILDFLOWERS

Project p. 14, 30 • Actual size

All embroidery floss is DMC No. 25; the number in parentheses is the number of strands.

C-3a (gray)	1. 809 (2)	C-2c (lavender)	1. 24 (2)
	2. 744 (2)		2. 153 (2)
	3. 165 (1) + 470 (1)		3. 3865 (1) + 3866 (1)
	4. 165 (2) + 470 (1)		4. 3865 (2) + 3866 (1)
C-2b (navy)	1. 304 (2)	C-2d (beige)	1. 3865 (2)
	2. 3864 (2)		2. 745 (2)
	3. 988 (1) + 3348 (1)		3. 472 (1) + 10 (1)
	4. 988 (2) + 3348 (1)		4. 472 (2) + 10 (1)

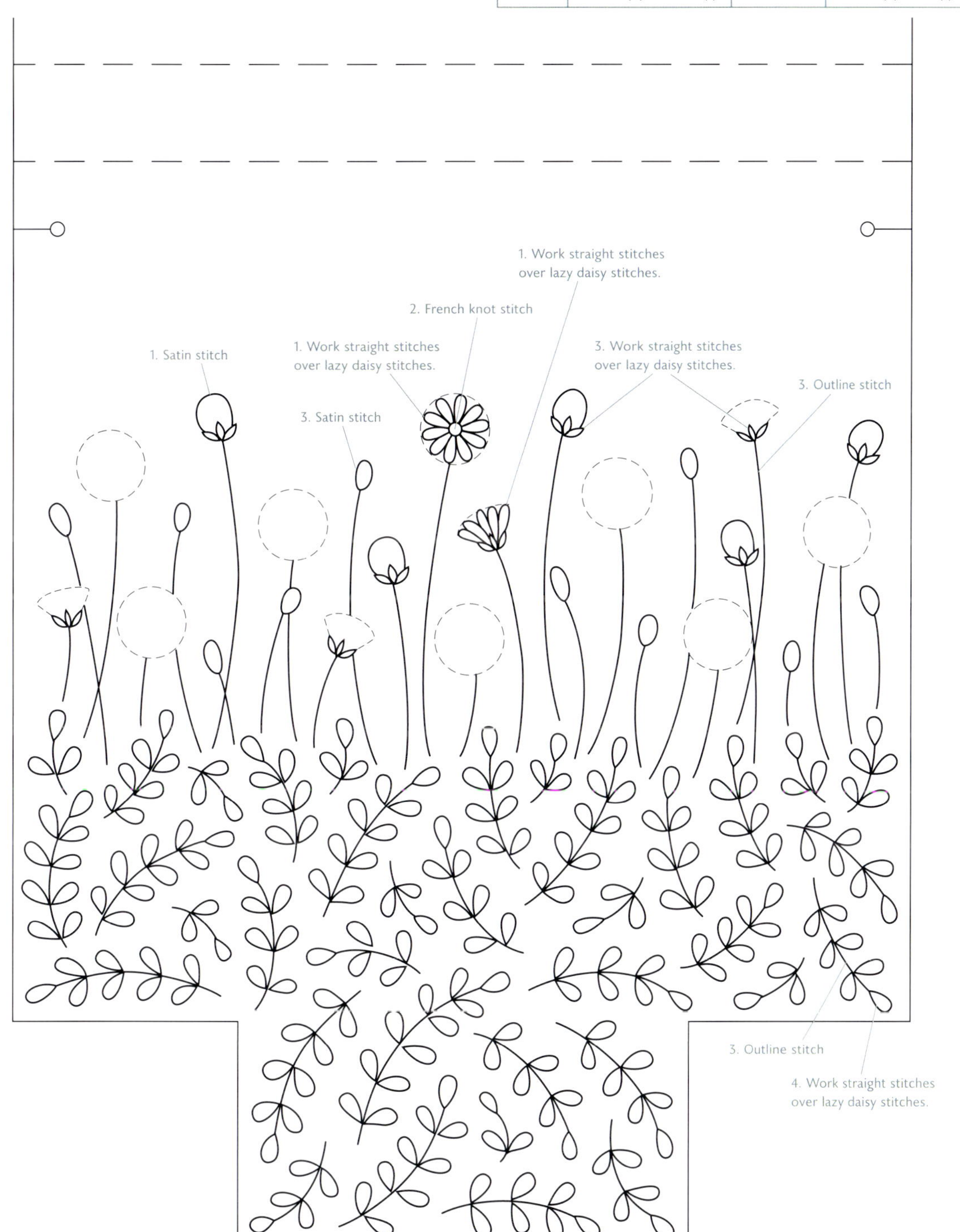

C-4A, B, C, D *JARDIN*

Project pp. 14, 31 • Actual size

All embroidery floss is DMC No. 25; the number in parentheses is the number of strands.

C-4a (brown)	1. 841 (2)	7. 840 (2)	13. 779 (3)	C-4c (gray)	1. 647 (2)	7. 535 (2)	13. 645 (3)
	2. 543 (2)	8. 840 (2)	14. 779 (2)		2. 3024 (2)	8. 535 (2)	14. 645 (2)
	3. 840 (3)	9. 3031 (3)	15. 632 (4)		3. 646 (3)	9. 3799 (3)	15. 648 (4)
	4. 842 (2)	10. 3782 (3)	16. 3858 (4)		4. 648 (2)	10. 646 (3)	16. 844 (4)
	5. 839 (2)	11. 3860 (2)	17. 3860 (3)		5. 3799 (2)	11. 413 (2)	17. 645 (3)
	6. 840 (3)	12. 3860 (2)			6. 535 (3)	12. 413 (2)	
C-4b (purple)	1. 3042 (2)	7. 451 (2)	13. 3861 (3)	C-4d (moss green)	1. 647 (2)	7. 502 (2)	13. 3787 (3)
	2. 3743 (2)	8. 3835 (2)	14. 3861 (2)		2. 3024 (2)	8. 502 (2)	14. 3787 (2)
	3. 3041 (3)	9. 3740 (3)	15. 3726 (4)		3. 3022 (3)	9. 501 (3)	15. 523 (4)
	4. 452 (2)	10. 452 (3)	16. 315 (4)		4. 3024 (2)	10. 3022 (3)	16. 522 (4)
	5. 3740 (2)	11. 3041 (2)	17. 3861 (3)		5. 501 (2)	11. 520 (2)	17. 523 (3)
	6. 451 (3)	12. 3041 (2)			6. 502 (3)	12. 520 (2)	

D-1 MINIATURE WREATH

Project p. 16 • Actual size

All embroidery floss is FUJIX, either Soie et or MOCO;
the number in parentheses is the number of strands.

D-2 BOTANICAL

Project p. 16 • Actual size

All embroidery floss is FUJIX: Soie et, MOCO, Sparkle Lame, or Sara; the number in parentheses is the number of strands.

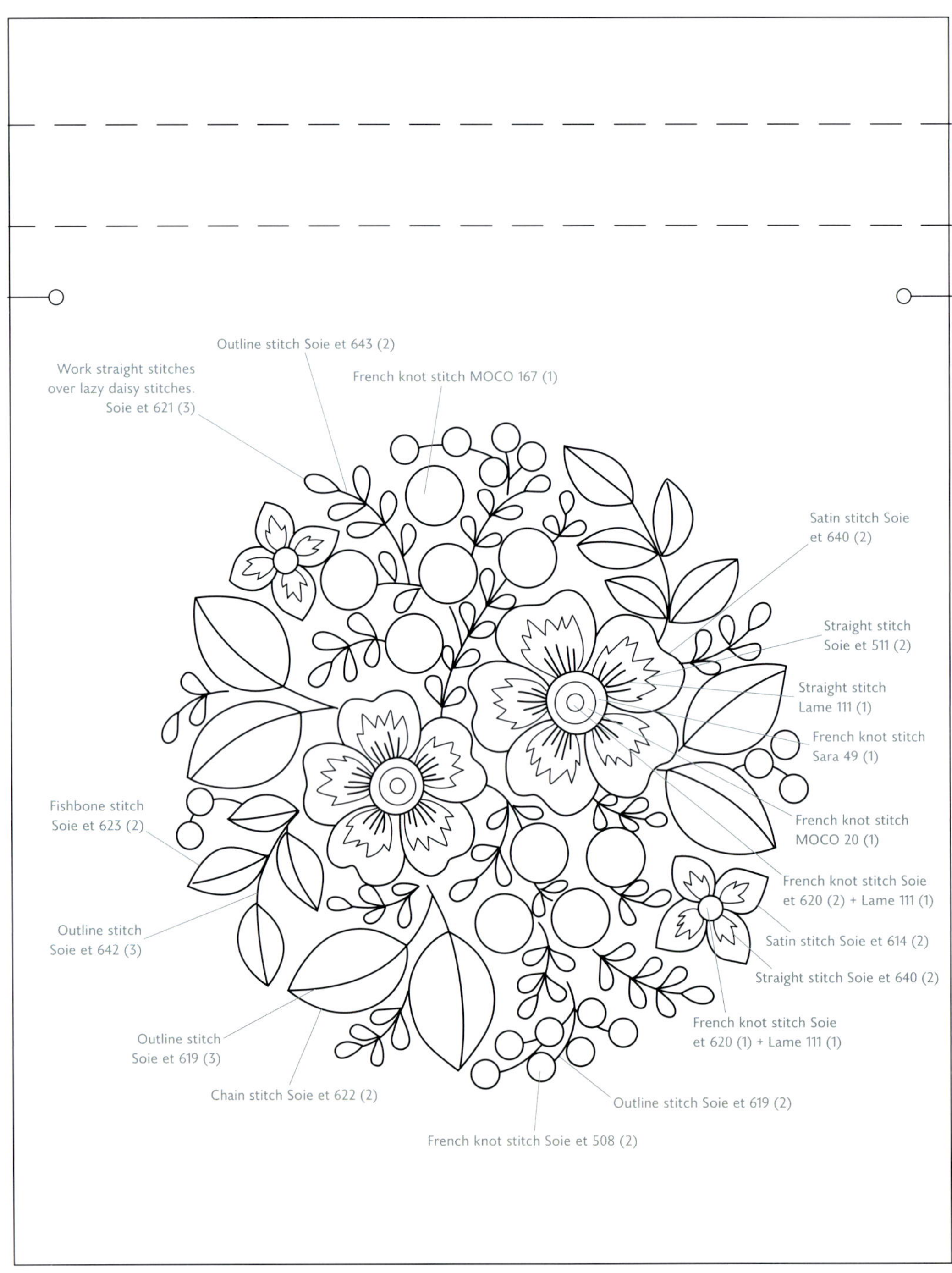

D-3 SUNLIGHT

Project p. 16 • Actual size

All embroidery floss is DMC No. 25; the number in parentheses is the number of strands.

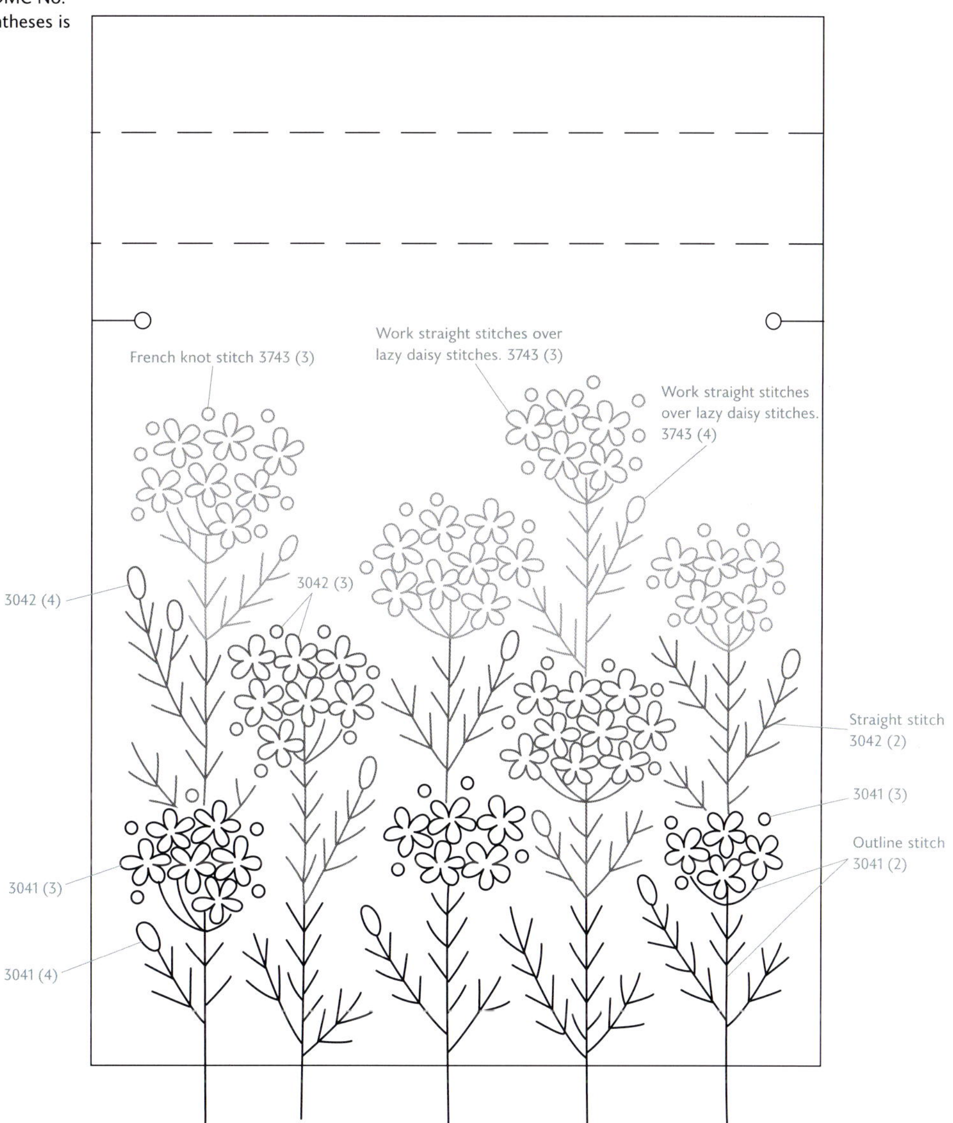

G•H-1A, B BLOOM

All embroidery floss is DMC No. 25; the number in parentheses is the number of strands. See page 84 for the patterns.

G•H-1a (dark green)	1. 309 (3)	7. 842 (3)	13. 3849 (2)	19. 3348 (2)	25. 562 (2)
	2. 745 (2)	8. 746 (2)	14. 712 (3)	20. 367 (3)	26. 746 (4)
	3. 3864 (3)	9. 677 (3)	15. 677 (2)	21. 367 (2)	27. 472 (2)
	4. 754 (2)	10. 402 (2)	16. 989 (2)	22. 739 (2)	
	5. 712 (2)	11. 745 (3)	17. 367 (2)	23. 3364 (2)	
	6. 3821 (3)	12. 10 (2)	18. 10 (2)	24. 562 (2)	

G•H-1b (navy)	1. 304 (3)	7. 754 (3)	13. 3849 (2)	19. 989 (2)	25. 772 (2)
	2. 677 (2)	8. 10 (2)	14. 746 (3)	20. 3348 (3)	26. 775 (4)
	3. 842 (3)	9. 677 (3)	15. 842 (2)	21. 3348 (2)	27. 3013 (2)
	4. ECRU (2)	10. 402 (2)	16. 987 (2)	22. ECRU (2)	
	5. 10 (2)	11. ECRU (3)	17. 471 (2)	23. 3347 (2)	
	6. 712 (3)	12. 677 (2)	18. 503 (2)	24. 772 (2)	

D-4A, B TREE

Project pp. 17, 31 • Actual size

All embroidery floss is DMC No. 25; "E" denotes lame thread, and the number in parentheses is the number of strands.

D-4a (black)	1. 3865 (2)
	2. 3865 (1) + E168 (1)
	3. 3865 (3)
	4. 3865 (2) + E168 (1)
	5. 3862 (2)

D-4b (red)	1. ECRU (2)
	2. ECRU (1) + E168 (1)
	3. ECRU (3)
	4. ECRU (2) + E168 (1)
	5. 3863 (2)

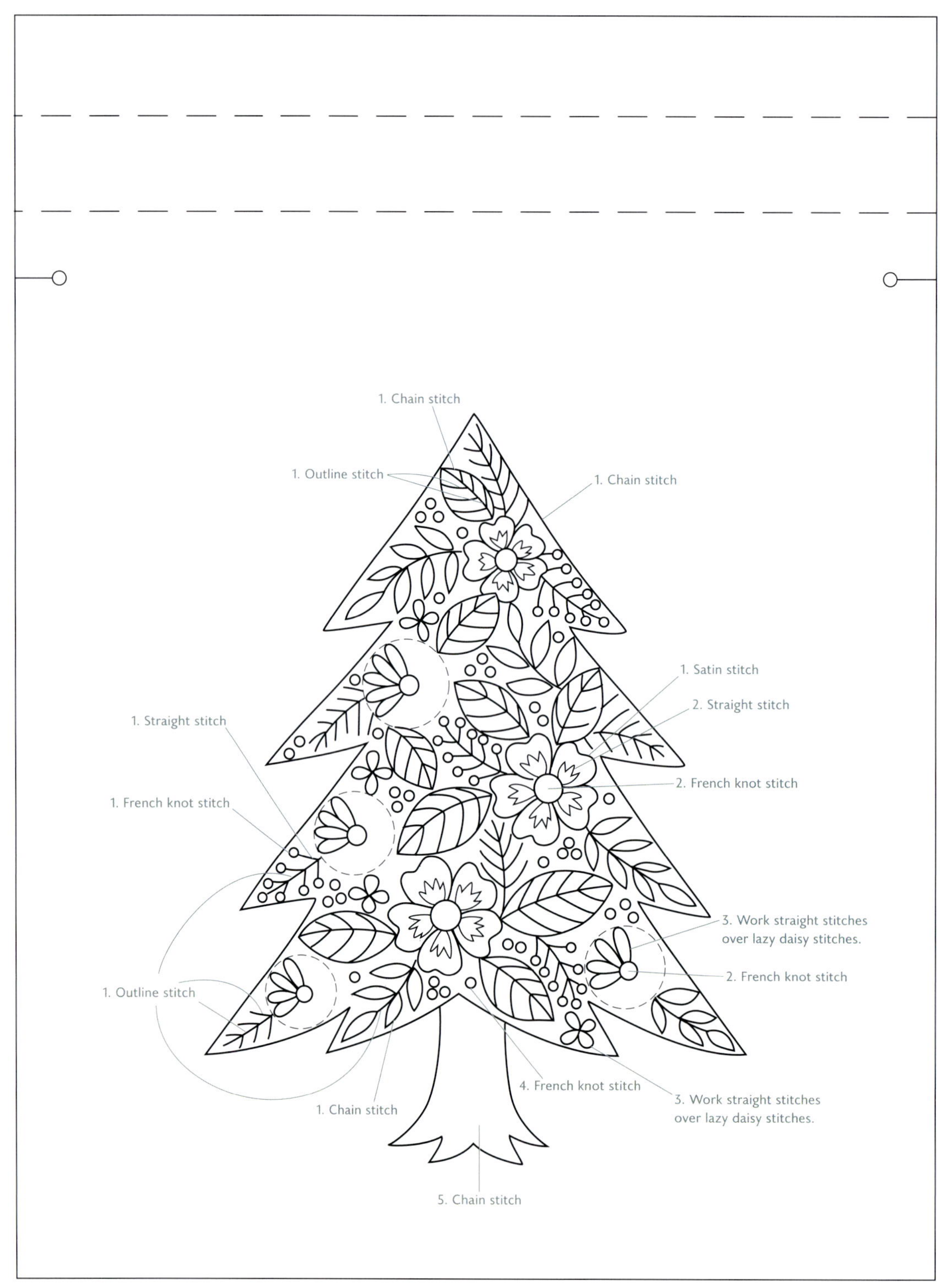

D-5a, b BOUQUET

Project p. 18 • Actual size

All embroidery floss is DMC No. 25; the number in parentheses is the number of strands.

D-5a (pink)	1. 151 (2)	7. 151 (3)	13. 3733 (2)	19. 151 (3)
	2. 760 (3)	8. 819 (2)	14. 819 (2)	20. 3326 (3)
	3. 819 (2)	9. 225 (2)	15. 961 (2)	21. 225 (3)
	4. 3326 (3)	10. 761 (2)	16. 961 (3)	22. 3326 (3)
	5. 3833 (3)	11. 760 (2)	17. 761 (2)	
	6. 225 (2)	12. 3733 (3)	18. 761 (3)	

D-5b (light blue)	1. 3755 (2)	7. 519 (3)	13. 3752 (2)	19. 3755 (3)
	2. 826 (3)	8. 3841 (2)	14. 828 (2)	20. 3841 (3)
	3. 3752 (2)	9. 519 (2)	15. 322 (2)	21. 3755 (3)
	4. 3325 (3)	10. 3752 (2)	16. 322 (3)	22. 3325 (3)
	5. 334 (3)	11. 3841 (2)	17. 826 (2)	
	6. 3752 (2)	12. 3752 (3)	18. 826 (3)	

Work straight stitches over lazy daisy stitches: K 19, L 4, M 5

French knot stitch: K 20, L 21, M 22

* See the corresponding letters on the pattern above.

G•H-1A, B BLOOM

Project p. 22 • Actual size

Embroidery floss chart p. 81

G•H-2A, B, C, D HYDRANGEAS

Project p. 32 • Actual size

All embroidery floss is DMC No. 25; the number in parentheses is the number of strands.

G•H-2a (black)	1. 712 (4)	2. 712 (3)	3. 3864 (2)	4. 3864 (1)
G•H-2b (khaki)	1. ECRU (4)	2. ECRU (3)	3. 3032 (2)	4. 3032 (1)
G•H-2c (light brown)	1. 543 (4)	2. 543 (3)	3. 3866 (2)	4. 3866 (1)
G•H-2d (blue)	1. 677 (4)	2. 677 (3)	3. 3364 (2)	4. 3364 (1)

G•H-3A, B RAINBOW EVERGREENS

Project p. 32 • Actual size

All embroidery floss is DMC No. 25; the number in parentheses is the number of strands.

*The color codes for the embroidery floss are the same for 3a and 3b. For the fabric, use navy for 3a and green for 3b.

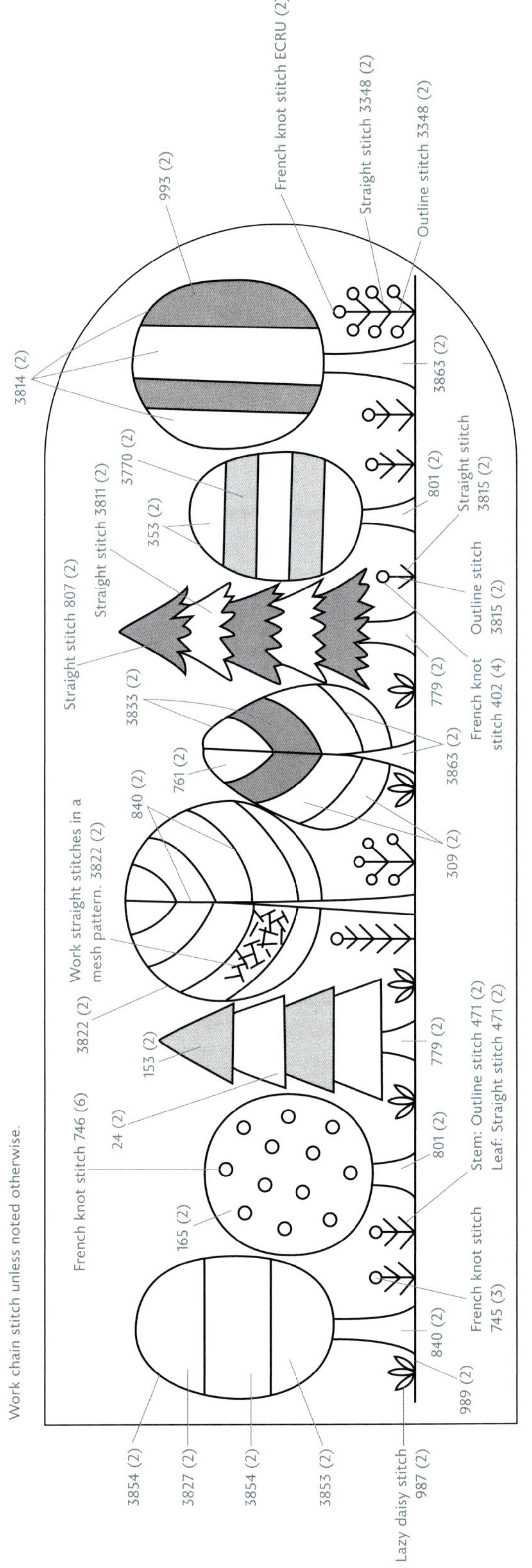

I-2A, B, C RIBBON BOUQUET

I-3A, B, C ETERNAL

I-4A, B, C CRESCENT

Project pp. 24, 25 • Actual size

All embroidery floss is DMC No. 25; the number in parentheses is the number of strands.

I-2a (light brown)	1. 746 (2)	2. 745 (3)	3. 746 (3)	4. 3013 (2)	5. 745 (2)	6. 3823 (2)
I-2b (navy)	1. 3865 (2)	2. 745 (3)	3. 3013 (3)	4. 3013 (2)	5. 353 (2)	6. 3770 (2)
I-2c (light blue)	1. 775 (2)	2. 3823 (3)	3. 3865 (3)	4. 3865 (2)	5. 3865 (2)	6. 519 (2)

I-3a (pink)	1. 3833 (3)	2. 761 (3)	3. 225 (2)
I-3b (light blue)	1. 518 (3)	2. 519 (3)	3. 3841 (2)
I-3c (yellow)	1. 745 (3)	2. 3823 (3)	3. 746 (2)

I-4a (brown)	1. 10 (2)	2. 745 (3)	3. 472 (2)	4. 10 (3)
I-4b (black)	1. 3865 (2)	2. 745 (3)	3. 561 (2)	4. 3865 (3)
I-4c (blue-gray)	1. ECRU (2)	2. 745 (3)	3. 3363 (2)	4. ECRU (3)

I-2

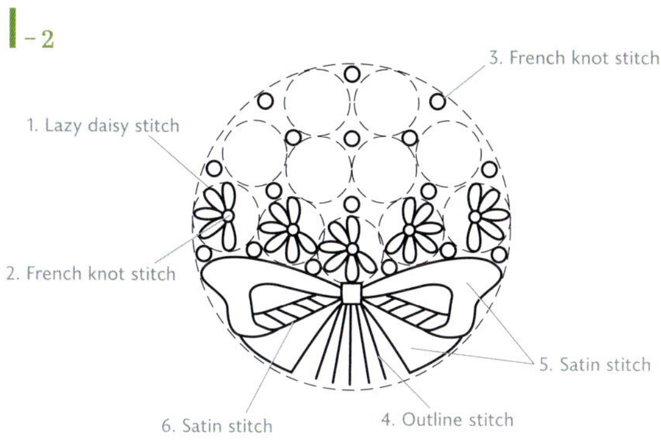

I-4

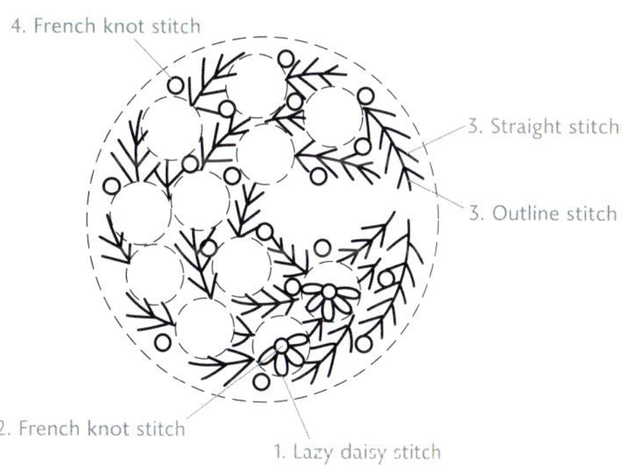

I-3

3. Work straight stitches over lazy daisy stitches.

3. Outline stitch

2. Outline stitch

1. Straight stitch

How to Stitch Miniature Roses

Refer to p. 37

Work straight stitches as shown above, then gradually round the edges.

Moving outward around the center, work overlapping outline stitches.

YULA

Yula is an embroidery artist. She graduated from fashion school and worked as a designer for an apparel company. After she got married, she started making handmade things as a hobby, and in 2016 she launched her Instagram with an emphasis on embroidery. Now, with over 100,000 followers, she continues to post regularly about her embroidery projects. Yula adores creating embroidery and needle arts projects with an attention to detail and vivid colors. Instagram: @yula_handmade_2008

Roost Books
An imprint of Shambhala Publications, Inc.
2129 13th Street
Boulder, Colorado 80302
www.roostbooks.com

Translation by Allison Markin Powell
Originally published as *Yura no shishuu: kusabana no shohousen* (NV70652) © 2021 by Yula / NIHON VOGUE-SHA

NIHON VOGUE STAFF CREDITS

Photographer: Tadaaki Ohomori
English translation rights arranged with NIHON VOGUE Corp. through Japan UNI Agency, Inc., Tokyo

9 8 7 6 5 4 3 2 1

First English edition
Printed in China

Shambhala Publications makes every effort to print on acid-free, recycled paper.
Shambhala Publications is distributed worldwide by Penguin Random House, Inc., and its subsidiaries.

Library of Congress Cataloging-in-Publication Data
Names: Yula (Embroidery artist) author
Title: Embroidering the magic of plants: healing flower, leaf, and herbal designs / Yula.
Description: Boulder: Roost Books, 2026. | Text in English and Japanese.
Identifiers: LCCN 2025031414 | ISBN 9781645474401 trade paperback
Subjects: LCSH: Embroidery—Patterns | Notions (Merchandise) | Flowers in art | Decoration and ornament—Plant forms
Classification: LCC TT771 .Y8513 2026
LC record available at https://lccn.loc.gov/2025031414

The authorized representative in the EU for product safety and compliance is eucomply OÜ, Pärnu mnt 139b-14, 11317 Tallinn, Estonia, hello@eucompliancepartner.com.